# BECOMING A GODLY MAN IN AN UNGODLY WORLD

Jody Burkeen

*Man Up God's Way*

*1729 W 5th Street*

*Eureka, MO 63025*
*www.manupgodsway.org*



*ISBN: 978-0-9839288-8-1*

*To order additional copies of the Becoming a Godly Man in an Ungodly World Workbook, or to explore other resources like Man Up – Becoming a Godly Man in an Ungodly World and Pursuit of a Godly Life – Living Like Jesus Matters, visit www.manupgodsway.org. You'll also find a variety of merchandise designed to support and equip you on your spiritual journey. To place your order, visit our website at www.manupgodsway.org or find our books and products on Amazon.*

# DEDICATION

To my beloved wife, Nan your unwavering support, love, and encouragement have been my anchor through this journey. You inspire me daily to be a better man, husband, and father. Thank you for standing beside me in our faith.

To my amazing children, Evee, Gabe, Addy, and Paul—each of you is a blessing. I pray that you continue to grow in your love for God and embrace His calling on your lives. I dedicate this work to you, hoping to leave a legacy of faith that guides you in the years to come.

To the church, I have the honor of pastoring—you have been a source of strength and a reminder of God's grace. Thank you for your commitment to walking this journey of faith with me.

And to all the men I have had the privilege to disciple—this work is for you. May you continue to rise to the challenge of godly manhood, walking boldly in faith and leading with Christ at the center of your lives.

## Daily Spiritual Disciplines: How to Read, Pray, and Repent Daily

One of the core principles of **Man Up God's Way** is the daily practice of three essential spiritual disciplines: reading your Bible, praying, and repenting of any sin that God reveals. These practices aren't just tasks to check off a list—they are powerful ways to connect with God, grow in faith, and stay in alignment with His will. Here's how you can make these three disciplines a part of your everyday routine:

### 1. Read Your Bible Daily

The Bible is your ultimate source of truth, wisdom, and guidance. It's how God speaks directly to you, revealing His will and helping you grow in your understanding of who He is and who He's called you to be. Here's how to approach it daily:

- **Set Aside Time:** Make reading your Bible a priority by scheduling time for it. Choose a consistent time that works for you, whether first thing in the morning, during lunch, or before bed.
- **Start Small:** If you're new to daily Bible reading, start with a manageable goal. You might read one chapter or follow a daily reading plan to guide you. Over time, you can increase the amount you read.
- **Pray for Understanding:** Before you open your Bible, ask God to reveal His truth to you and help you apply it to your life. The Holy Spirit will guide you as you read.
- **Meditate on a Verse:** As you read, take time to meditate on a specific verse or passage. Think about how it applies to your life and how God is speaking to you through it.

### 2. Pray Daily

Prayer is your direct line of communication with God. It's how you build your relationship with Him, share your heart, and seek His guidance. Here's how to establish a consistent prayer life:

- **Keep It Simple:** Prayer doesn't have to be complicated. Talk to God openly and honestly about your concerns, joys, and needs.
- **Make it a Habit:** Begin and end your day with prayer. Set aside specific times to connect with God throughout the day, whether it's during a quiet moment or while you're driving.

- **Use a Prayer Guide:** If you're unsure where to start, use the ACTS model—Adoration, Confession, Thanksgiving, and Supplication—to guide your prayers.
- **Listen:** Prayer is a two-way conversation. After you talk to God, take time to listen to what He may be saying to you, whether it's through Scripture or a quiet impression on your heart.

### 3. Repent of Any Sin God Reveals

Repentance is a vital part of spiritual growth. It means turning away from sin and turning toward God. When you ask the Holy Spirit to reveal sin in your life, you allow God to cleanse and restore you. Here's how to make repentance a regular part of your day:

- **Examine Your Heart:** Spend time each day asking God to show you areas in your life where sin may be hindering your relationship with Him. This could be a thought, an attitude, or an action.
- **Confess Your Sin:** When God reveals sin, don't ignore it. Confess it to Him immediately. Be honest about where you've fallen short and ask for His forgiveness.
- **Turn Away from Sin:** Repentance isn't just about saying sorry; it's about making a change. Ask God to help you turn away from sinful behaviors and replace them with godly actions.
- **Seek Accountability:** If there's a recurring sin in your life, don't be afraid to seek help from a trusted brother in Christ. Accountability can help you stay on the path of righteousness.

### Make These Disciplines a Habit

Building these three disciplines—reading your Bible, praying, and repenting daily—takes intentionality and discipline. But as you practice them consistently, you'll find that your relationship with God deepens, your spiritual strength grows, and you become better equipped to face the challenges of life as a godly man. Start today. Commit to making these practices a part of your everyday routine and watch how God transforms your life.

# TABLE OF CONTENTS

# INTRODUCTION

Welcome to **Becoming a Godly Man in an Ungodly World Workbook**, a resource designed to help you grow deeper in your relationship with God and embrace the high calling of biblical manhood. In a world that constantly challenges what it means to be a man, this workbook will guide you through Scripture and practical applications, helping you stand firm in your faith and live with purpose in every area of life.

## Why This Discipleship Workbook?

As Christian men, we face unique challenges in today's culture. Society promotes definitions of manhood that are often far from God's design. We are told that success is found in power, wealth, or status, but God calls us to a different path—a path of humility, sacrifice, and service. The journey of becoming a godly man is not easy, but it is necessary to live lives that honor Christ and leave a lasting impact on those around us.

This workbook is built around the foundation laid in the Amazon Best-selling book **Man Up- Becoming a Godly Man in an Ungodly World**, but it takes the principles even deeper. It's designed to not just inspire you but to give you the tools, structure, and accountability to apply these biblical truths in your daily life. The goal is to equip you to take actionable steps toward being the man God has called you to be.

## How to Use This Workbook

This workbook is divided into sections that reflect the key growth areas in biblical manhood: spiritual discipline, leadership, overcoming temptation, and more. Each chapter provides:

- **Key Scriptures:** These are the foundation of everything you'll be studying. Each section will guide you through critical passages highlighting God's blueprint for manhood.
- **Discussion and Reflection Questions:** These are designed to help you process and apply what you've learned to your own life. Take time to reflect on your answers honestly.

- **Action Steps:** It's not enough to read about biblical manhood—you need to live it out. Each section includes practical steps to grow spiritually and lead effectively.
- **Man Up Challenges:** These challenges are meant to push you beyond your comfort zone and encourage you to live out your faith boldly. Each challenge will call you to step up in a specific area of your life.

I encourage you to approach this workbook prayerfully. Ask God to reveal areas where you need to grow, whether it's in your personal spiritual habits, your leadership in the home, or your influence at work. Be open to His leading and be willing to act on what He shows you.

## Accountability and Brotherhood

As you go through this workbook, please don't do it alone. Biblical manhood is meant to be lived in community with other godly men. Proverbs 27:17 says, "*As iron sharpens iron, so one person sharpens another.*" You need accountability—men who will walk alongside you, encourage you, challenge you, and pray for you.

If you're part of a men's group, use the material in this workbook as a tool for group discussion and growth. Share openly, hold each other accountable, and push one another toward spiritual maturity. If you're going through this workbook alone, I challenge you to find a brother in Christ who can hold you accountable for your commitments.

## What You Will Gain

By working through this material, you will understand what it means to live as a godly man in today's world. You will learn how to lead your family with Christlike love, how to stand firm in your faith in the face of temptation, and how to pursue spiritual disciplines that keep you grounded in God's Word. Most importantly, you will be equipped to make an impact for the Kingdom of God in your home, your church, and your community.

This journey will not be without challenges. There will be moments when you are tested, and you may even feel discouraged. But remember, God is faithful. Philippians 1:6 says, "[6] *For I am* confident of this very thing, that He who began a good work in you will perfect it until the day of Christ Jesus." Trust in His work in your life, and don't give up when the road gets tough. Persevere, and you will see the fruit of godliness growing in every area of your life.

### A Call to Action

This is more than just a workbook—it's a call to action. It's a challenge for you to rise up and embrace the role of a godly man in a world that desperately needs you to stand strong in your faith. It's time to reject passivity, take responsibility, and lead with courage. The world is watching, your family is watching, and God is calling you to be the man He created you to be. Are you ready to Man Up God's Way? Let's get started.

**In Christ,**

Jody Burkeen

Founder, Man Up God's Way

# LEADER'S GUIDE FOR USING THIS WORKBOOK AND ACCOUNTABILITY QUESTIONS

## Overview

This workbook is designed as a practical tool to help men grow spiritually, understand God's calling, and live out biblical principles in every aspect of life. Each chapter covers a different topic essential for building a godly character, from understanding identity in Christ to leading your family and overcoming temptation. As a leader, your role is to guide the group through each chapter, encourage **open and honest** discussions, be honest yourself, and hold members accountable in a spirit of love and humility.

## How to Use the Workbook

1. **Prepare in Advance**
    - **Review the Chapter Content**: Familiarize yourself with each chapter's main points, Scriptures, and objectives. This will help you guide discussions effectively and offer deeper insights.
    - **Pray for Guidance**: Before each meeting, pray for wisdom and for the Holy Spirit's guidance to lead the group in a way that honors God and fosters growth.
    - **Study the Accountability Questions**: Read through the accountability questions at the end of each chapter and consider how to present them in a way that encourages reflection and genuine sharing.
2. **Set Expectations for the Group**
    - **Encourage Consistent Attendance**: Emphasize the importance of commitment to the group for personal growth and the benefit of the other men.

- **Establish Confidentiality**: Create a safe environment by establishing that what is shared stays in the group, encouraging vulnerability and openness.

- **Foster Accountability**: Let the group know that accountability is a vital part of the journey. The questions at the end of each chapter help each man examine his heart and actions in a supportive and non-judgmental setting.

3. **Structure Each Meeting**

- **Opening Prayer**: Begin each session with prayer, inviting God's presence and asking for hearts open to growth and change.

- **Chapter Discussion**: Guide the group through the chapter content, encouraging participation and insights. Allow men to share personal experiences related to the topic and ask follow-up questions to deepen the discussion.

- **Scripture Exploration**: Spend time reading and reflecting on the key Scriptures in each chapter. Discuss how these verses apply to each man's life and what challenges or insights they reveal.

- **Accountability Questions**: At the end of each chapter, go through the accountability questions together. Encourage honest reflection on each question, inviting each man to share his answers to the extent he feels comfortable. This is invaluable and should be the highlight of each meeting.

4. **Using the Accountability Questions Effectively**

- **Encourage Transparency**: Remind group members that the accountability questions are meant to prompt self-examination and growth, not to create guilt or shame. Honesty and humility will lead to the greatest transformation.

- **Promote Practical Application**: Encourage each man to consider specific steps to respond to the questions. For example, if a question focuses on spiritual disciplines, ask how each man plans to integrate those practices into his week.

- **Offer Encouragement and Prayer**: Accountability questions can reveal struggles and challenges. After each question, provide time for group members to encourage and pray for each other. Remind everyone that no one is on this journey alone.

5. **Follow-Up and Check-In**

   - **Weekly Check-In**: At the start of each new session, take a few minutes to ask how everyone did with the previous week's commitments. Encourage each man to share any progress or obstacles they encountered.

   - **One-on-One Follow-Up**: Occasionally check in with group members individually to offer further support and prayer. This can help reinforce accountability and provide a space for deeper sharing outside the group setting.

   - **Start a text thread**: Check on your group through text. Follow up each week to make sure each man is staying committed to

6. **Encourage Ongoing Growth Beyond the Workbook**

   - Remind the group that the principles learned in this workbook are intended to be lifelong practices. Encourage each man to continue seeking God, applying these lessons, and engaging with accountability partners even after completing the study.

## Tips for Success

- **Lead by Example**: Be open about your own journey and struggles. When the leader is transparent and authentic, it encourages the group to be transparent and authentic.

- **Create a Balance**: Encourage both depth in spiritual growth and practical application. Remind the group that biblical principles are meant to transform both our hearts and our actions.

- **Celebrate Progress**: Acknowledge each man's commitment to growth. Celebrate steps forward, no matter how small, and remind the group that spiritual growth is a process.

- **Pray Consistently**: Pray regularly for each group member's growth and strength. Encourage the men to pray for one another, building a community that supports each other's spiritual journeys.

# USER'S GUIDE

## Welcome to Your Journey of Growth and Accountability

This workbook is designed to guide you through a series of studies and reflections that will help you deepen your faith, develop godly character, and grow in your relationship with others. Each chapter addresses a core aspect of the Christian life, providing practical steps and insights to apply to your everyday walk with God. Following the guide will help you make the most out of each section and embrace the process of genuine accountability.

## Using the Workbook in Group Settings

1. **Prepare Ahead**

    - **Read the Chapter**: Before each group meeting, take time to read through the chapter carefully. Reflect on the key points and consider how they apply to your own life. Being prepared will help you contribute meaningfully to group discussions.

    - **Complete the Exercises**: Each chapter contains questions, reflections, and prompts to help you apply the material to your life. Take time to complete these exercises honestly, as they will serve as a foundation for meaningful discussion.

2. **Engage Actively in Group Discussions**

    - **Listen and Respect**: Group discussions work best when everyone listens respectfully. When someone is sharing, listen actively, and remember that each person's journey is unique.

    - **Share Honestly**: This is a safe space to be open about your struggles, victories, and growth. Don't hold back from sharing because of fear or shame. True growth happens in honesty.

- ❍ **Encourage One Another**: The purpose of the group is to build each other up. Offer words of encouragement, pray for one another, and remind each other of God's grace and strength.

3. **Commit to Weekly Accountability**

- ❍ **Review Accountability Questions**: At the end of each chapter, you'll find a set of accountability questions. These questions are designed to prompt self-reflection and honest assessment of your progress. Before the meeting, take time to answer these questions thoughtfully.
- ❍ **Share Your Answers**: During group time, you'll have the opportunity to share your answers with the group or a designated accountability partner. Be as open as possible, sharing not only your victories but also areas where you struggle. Remember, everyone in the group is on a journey, and no one is perfect.
- ❍ **Celebrate Progress, No Matter How Small**: Growth is a process. Celebrate the steps you've taken, even if they seem small. Each step forward is a victory.

4. **Confidentiality is Key**

- ❍ **Respect Privacy**: What's shared in the group stays in the group. Trust is essential for open and honest sharing. Honor the privacy of each member and keep all shared information confidential.
- ❍ **Build Trust Through Consistency**: Show up consistently and be dependable. The more each member can rely on one another, the stronger the bond and the deeper the growth.

## Answering the Accountability Questions Honestly

1. **Reflect Prayerfully**

- ❍ **Seek God's Guidance**: Begin by praying and asking God to reveal areas in your life that need growth. Ask for wisdom to see where you need to improve and for the courage to be honest with yourself and the group.
- ❍ **Examine Yourself with Humility**: Take time to reflect on each question. Be humble and willing to see both your strengths and areas for improvement. Let the Holy Spirit guide you into truth as you answer each question.

2. **Embrace Vulnerability**

   - **Be Honest About Weaknesses**: It's easy to talk about our strengths, but true growth happens when we're willing to confront our weaknesses. Answering the questions honestly means acknowledging areas where you're struggling or need more discipline. Remember, everyone faces challenges, and this is a place to be real.

   - **Celebrate Wins and Progress**: Don't hesitate to share your progress, no matter how small. Celebrating victories, even minor ones, is essential for building confidence and momentum.

3. **Accept Accountability**

   - **Allow Others to Hold You Accountable**: Accountability questions are designed to bring out areas where you might need extra support. Be open to constructive feedback and encouragement from your group. Let others speak into your life as you work to overcome challenges.

   - **Commit to Weekly Follow-Through**: At the end of each week, revisit your answers and evaluate your progress. Are you moving in the direction you want to go? Use each week's answers as motivation to keep growing.

4. **Seek Continuous Improvement**

   - **Make Practical Changes**: Each week, identify one or two practical steps you can take to improve in specific areas. Use your accountability questions as a guide for setting small, achievable goals that will help you develop consistency.

   - **Remember Grace**: Growth doesn't happen overnight, and setbacks are part of the process. Extend grace to yourself and remember that God's love and strength are always available to help you get back on track.

5. **Pray for One Another**

   - **End Each Meeting in Prayer**: After discussing accountability questions, close your group time by praying for each other's growth, challenges, and victories. Ask God to strengthen each member, provide guidance, and continue working in each person's heart.

## Making the Most of the Workbook

- **Focus on Application, Not Just Information**: This workbook aims to help you apply biblical principles to your daily life. Rather than just reading through, consider how each lesson can transform how you live. Use this workbook as a supplement to your daily bible reading and study.
- **Follow Up During the Week**: Keep in touch with your group or accountability partner between meetings. Send a message or check in to offer support, encouragement, and accountability.
- **Reflect on Progress**: Review previous chapters and see how far you've come. Reflecting on progress can help you stay motivated and remind you of God's work.
- **Year Through the Bible**: During the week, you are encouraged to read your Bible daily. There is a daily reading plan to follow that if read consistently, you will finish the Bible in a year.

# CHAPTER 1
# FOUNDATION OF BIBLICAL MANHOOD

# FOUNDATION OF BIBLICAL MANHOOD

## WEEK 1: CREATED IN GOD'S IMAGE

From the very beginning of the Bible, we learn something incredible about ourselves—we are made in the image of God. This truth is foundational to understanding who we are as men and how we are called to live. Being created in God's image means that our lives have a unique and sacred purpose. It means we are called to reflect God's character, live according to His design, and represent Him in every aspect of our lives.

But what does it truly mean to be made in the image of God? In a world that constantly pushes false definitions of manhood—whether it's success, power, or independence—God offers us a different, more fulfilling purpose. He calls us to live in a way that reflects His glory, embracing our role as image-bearers.

This week, we will dive into what it means to live as men who reflect God's image. We'll explore how being created in His likeness influences our relationships, our work, our identity, and our mission in life. You'll be challenged to look at yourself differently—not as the world defines you, but as God defines you.

As we begin, take some time to think about how being made in God's image affects the way you see yourself and the way you live. Let this truth shape your identity and guide your actions this week as we explore this foundational principle of biblical manhood.

- **Focus:** Understanding what it means to be made in God's image.
- **Key Scripture:** Genesis 1:26-27

> *"[26] Then God said, "Let Us make man in Our image, according to Our likeness; and let them rule over the fish of the sea and over the birds of the sky and over the cattle and over all the earth, and over every creeping thing that creeps on the earth." [27] God created man in His own image, in the image of God He created him; male and female He created them."*

- Discussion Questions:

1. What does being made in God's image mean for how we live as men?

_______________________________________________

_______________________________________________

_______________________________________________

_______________________________________________

_______________________________________________

2. How should this affect our relationships, work, and purpose in life?

_______________________________________________

_______________________________________________

_______________________________________________

_______________________________________________

_______________________________________________

3. What is the image you see in the mirror? Your past? Your future? Jesus?

_______________________________________________

_______________________________________________

_______________________________________________

_______________________________________________

- **Action Step:** Reflect on how your life reflects the image of God. Write down three ways you can intentionally represent Christ in your daily life.

- **Man Up Challenge:** Start each day this week with a prayer of surrender to God, asking Him to help you live out your identity as His image-bearer.

Each week, you will have a reading plan to help you read through the Bible in one year, while doing your group work. The goal is to get you in the Bible every day!

**Daily Bible Reading for Week 1:** *Genesis 1–11; Matthew 1–4*

**Week 1 Accountability Questions for You and/ or Your Group: (End each week, holding each other accountable with these questions. Be honest, this is where we grow.)**

| | | Yes | No |
|---|---|---|---|
| 1. | Have you spent daily time in the Scriptures and in prayer? | | |
| 2. | Have you had any impure thoughts that would not glorify God? | | |
| 3. | Have you been completely above reproach in your financial dealings? | | |
| 4. | Have you spent quality relationship time with family and friends? | | |
| 5. | Have you done your 100% best in your job, school, home, etc.? | | |
| 6. | Have you told any half-truths or outright lies, putting yourself in a better light to those around you? | | |
| 7. | Have you shared the Gospel with an unbeliever this week? | | |
| 8. | Have you taken care of your body through daily physical exercise and proper eating/sleeping habits? | | |
| 9. | Have you allowed any person or circumstance to rob you of your joy? | | |
| 10. | Have you lied on any of your answers today? | | |

**Prayer Request**

- ______________________________
- ______________________________
- ______________________________
- ______________________________
- ______________________________
- ______________________________
- ______________________________

**Name 5 People To Pray for this Week**

- ______________________________
- ______________________________
- ______________________________
- ______________________________
- ______________________________
- ______________________________
- ______________________________

Each week, we will give you men in the Bible who exemplified the main theme. Take time this week to study these men.

**1. Adam – The First Image Bearer**

- **Scripture:** Genesis 1:26-27; Genesis 2:7
- **Overview:** Adam was the first man created in the image of God. His creation reveals the uniqueness of humanity, made to reflect God's nature, and highlights the responsibility given to man to steward God's creation.

**2. Joseph – A Man of Integrity and Purpose**

- **Scripture:** Genesis 39:2-6; Genesis 50:19-20
- **Overview:** Joseph's life demonstrates how being made in the image of God involves living with integrity, even in difficult circumstances. Despite betrayal and hardship, Joseph reflected God's character through his forgiveness and leadership.

**3. David – A Man After God's Own Heart**

- **Scripture:** 1 Samuel 13:14; Psalm 139:13-16
- **Overview:** David is described as a man after God's own heart. His life, though marked by failures, reflects the pursuit of a deep relationship with God and an understanding of his own identity in God's design.

> *"To be made in the image of God means that we reflect His character and purpose in everything we do. It is our calling to represent Him in every area of life."* — **Tim Keller**

# MANHOOD AND RESPONSIBILITY

## WEEK 2: MANHOOD AND RESPONSIBILITY

One of the defining characteristics of biblical manhood is the call to take responsibility. From the beginning, when God created Adam, He entrusted him with responsibility—responsibility for the earth, responsibility for his work, and responsibility for his family. This call to responsible leadership is woven into the fabric of what it means to be a man created in God's image.

In today's world, responsibility is often shrugged off or neglected. Society may push men to pursue selfish goals, seek comfort, or avoid the hard work of leading well. But God's design for men is clear: true manhood is rooted in taking responsibility for what God has entrusted to us. This includes our families, our work, our communities, and most importantly, our spiritual lives.

This week, we will explore what it means to embrace responsibility as a man of God. We'll look at how Adam's responsibility in the Garden of Eden reflects our own roles as caretakers, protectors, and leaders today. Whether it's leading your family in faith, being diligent in your work, or standing up for truth in your community, the call to take responsibility is central to living out biblical manhood.

As we study God's Word this week, ask yourself: Am I stepping up to the responsibilities God has placed in my life? How can I lead with greater courage and conviction in the areas where He has called me to serve?

The challenge before you is to reject passivity and embrace the God-given role of responsibility. Let this week inspire you to grow as a man who takes ownership of his calling and leads with strength and integrity.

- **Focus:** Embracing biblical responsibility as a man.
- **Key Scripture:** Genesis 1:28

> *"[8] God blessed them; and God said to them, "Be fruitful and multiply, and fill the earth, and subdue it; and rule over the fish of the sea and over the birds of the sky and over every living thing that moves on the earth." '"*

- Discussion Questions:

1. What responsibilities were given to Adam in the Garden of Eden, and how do they apply today?

2. How can we balance work, family, and spiritual responsibilities as godly men?

3. What responsibilities do you think you are lacking? At Home? At Work? At Church?

- **Action Step:** Identify areas in your life where you need to take more responsibility (family, work, spiritual life). Write out an action plan for growth in one of these areas.

- **Man Up Challenge:** Take ownership of one responsibility this week that you have been neglecting and seek to honor God through it.

**Week 2 Bible Reading***: Genesis 12–24; Matthew 5–7*

**Week 2 Accountability Questions for You and/ or Your Group: (End each week, holding each other accountable with these questions. Be honest, this is where we grow.)**

| | | Yes | No |
|---|---|---|---|
| 1. | Have you spent daily time in the Scriptures and in prayer? | | |
| 2. | Have you had any impure thoughts that would not glorify God? | | |
| 3. | Have you been completely above reproach in your financial dealings? | | |
| 4. | Have you spent quality relationship time with family and friends? | | |
| 5. | Have you done your 100% best in your job, school, home, etc.? | | |
| 6. | Have you told any half-truths or outright lies, putting yourself in a better light to those around you? | | |
| 7. | Have you shared the Gospel with an unbeliever this week? | | |
| 8. | Have you taken care of your body through daily physical exercise and proper eating/sleeping habits? | | |
| 9. | Have you allowed any person or circumstance to rob you of your joy? | | |
| 10. | Have you lied on any of your answers today? | | |

**Prayer Request**

- ______________________
- ______________________
- ______________________
- ______________________
- ______________________
- ______________________
- ______________________

**Name 5 People To Pray for this Week**

- ______________________
- ______________________
- ______________________
- ______________________
- ______________________
- ______________________
- ______________________

Each week, we will give you men in the Bible who exemplified the main theme. Take time this week to study these men.

**1. Noah – Faithful in Responsibility**

- Scripture: Genesis 6:9-22; Genesis 7:5
- Overview: Noah took responsibility for following God's command to build the ark, even when it seemed impossible and unreasonable. His obedience saved his family and preserved humanity. Noah's story shows the importance of trusting God and taking responsibility in difficult situations.

**2. Joshua – Responsible for Leading God's People**

- Scripture: Joshua 1:1-9
- Overview: After Moses' death, Joshua was called to take responsibility for leading the Israelites into the Promised Land. God commanded him to be strong and courageous as he stepped into this enormous role. Joshua's faith and leadership demonstrated a deep sense of responsibility.

**3. Boaz – A Responsible Protector and Provider**

- Scripture: Ruth 2:1-12; Ruth 4:9-10
- Overview: Boaz took responsibility for protecting and providing for Ruth, a vulnerable widow, despite not being obligated to do so. His actions reflect godly character and responsibility toward family and community.

> *"A godly man takes responsibility for his actions, his family, and his faith. He doesn't make excuses—he steps up, takes the lead, and follows God's design for his life."*
> **— Jody Burkeen**

# STRENGTH AND COURAGE IN BIBLICAL MANHOOD

## WEEK 3: STRENGTH AND COURAGE IN BIBLICAL MANHOOD

Being a man of strength and courage doesn't just mean physical power or bravery in the face of danger. True biblical manhood calls for a deeper, spiritual strength and courage that comes from trusting in God's power and standing firm in the truth, even when the world is pushing in the opposite direction. In today's culture, where compromise and passivity often define masculinity, God calls us to stand firm, to be courageous, and to act with boldness grounded in our faith.

This week, we will explore what it means to live with the strength and courage that come from knowing Christ. The world offers a distorted view of manhood, where strength is often measured by power, status, or independence. But in the Bible, true strength comes from humility, submission to God, and the courage to live out your convictions in every area of life—whether leading your family, standing up for righteousness, or remaining faithful in the face of adversity.

We'll be diving into the example of Jesus, who displayed incredible strength through service, sacrifice, and love. We will also look at how God's Word equips us to be courageous men of faith, who lead with integrity and boldness in a world that often rejects biblical truth.

As you work through this week, ask yourself: Where do I need to show greater strength and courage in my life? In what areas have I allowed fear, doubt, or passivity to keep me from living as the man God has called me to be?

Let this week challenge you to rely on God's strength and step boldly into the roles He has given you. God has not called you to a life of timidity but of power, love, and self-discipline. Let's dig into what it means to be a man of strength and courage in Christ.

- **Focus:** Developing strength and courage in your walk as a man of God.
- **Key Scripture:** 1 Corinthians 16:13-14

> *"13 Be on the alert, stand firm in the faith, act like men, be strong. 14 Let all that you do be done in love."*

- Discussion Questions:

1. What does it mean to "act like men" according to this scripture?

______________________________________________

______________________________________________

______________________________________________

______________________________________________

______________________________________________

2. How can we balance strength and love in our daily lives?

______________________________________________

______________________________________________

______________________________________________

______________________________________________

______________________________________________

3. Am I engaging in the Bible daily? If not, why? Can I become the man I need to be without it?

______________________________________________

______________________________________________

______________________________________________

______________________________________________

______________________________________________

- **Action Step:** Commit to stand firm in one area of your life where you have struggled to act with spiritual strength. Write your commitment/s down here.

- **Man Up Challenge:** Identify one area of your life that requires more courage (e.g., sharing your faith, leading your family). Pray daily for the courage to stand firm and take action in that area.

**Week 3 Bible Reading**: *Genesis 25–36; Matthew 8–10*

**Week 3 Accountability Questions for You and/ or Your Group: (End each week, holding each other accountable with these questions. Be honest, this is where we grow.)**

| | | Yes | No |
|---|---|---|---|
| 1. | Have you spent daily time in the Scriptures and in prayer? | | |
| 2. | Have you had any impure thoughts that would not glorify God? | | |
| 3. | Have you been completely above reproach in your financial dealings? | | |
| 4. | Have you spent quality relationship time with family and friends? | | |
| 5. | Have you done your 100% best in your job, school, home, etc.? | | |
| 6. | Have you told any half-truths or outright lies, putting yourself in a better light to those around you? | | |
| 7. | Have you shared the Gospel with an unbeliever this week? | | |
| 8. | Have you taken care of your body through daily physical exercise and proper eating/sleeping habits? | | |
| 9. | Have you allowed any person or circumstance to rob you of your joy? | | |
| 10. | Have you lied on any of your answers today? | | |

| **Prayer Request** | **Name 5 People To Pray for this Week** |
|---|---|
| • ______________________ | • ______________________ |
| • ______________________ | • ______________________ |
| • ______________________ | • ______________________ |
| • ______________________ | • ______________________ |
| • ______________________ | • ______________________ |
| • ______________________ | • ______________________ |
| • ______________________ | • ______________________ |

Each week, we will give you men in the Bible who exemplified the main theme. Take time this week to study these men.

1. **David – Courage to Face Goliath**
    - Scripture: 1 Samuel 17:32-37, 1 Samuel 17:45-50
    - Overview: David showed extraordinary courage and strength when he faced Goliath, trusting not in his own abilities but in God's power to deliver victory. David's faith in God empowered him to take on a seemingly impossible challenge.
2. **Gideon – Courage to Lead in Weakness**
    - Scripture: Judges 6:11-16; Judges 7:7-21
    - Overview: Gideon was called by God to lead Israel against the Midianites, even though he felt inadequate. Despite his doubts and fears, Gideon's strength came from God, and he led a small army to victory. His story shows that true courage comes from relying on God, not on our own strength.
3. **Joshua – Strength to Lead with God's Promise**
    - Scripture: Joshua 1:6-9
    - Overview: After the death of Moses, Joshua was tasked with leading the Israelites into the Promised Land. God repeatedly encouraged Joshua to be strong and courageous, reminding him that His presence would go with him. Joshua's strength came from trusting in God's promises and following His commands.

> *"Courage is not simply one of the virtues, but the form of every virtue at the testing point."* — **C.S. Lewis**

# DAILY COMMITMENT TO GOD'S DESIGN

## WEEK 4: DAILY COMMITMENT TO GOD'S DESIGN

True spiritual growth doesn't happen in occasional bursts or in just the monumental moments of life—it's the result of consistent, daily commitment to God's design for your life. Being a godly man means that each day you choose to live according to His Word, seeking His will in the big decisions and the small, often unnoticed moments. This kind of commitment requires discipline, perseverance, and trust in God's plan even when it feels difficult or inconvenient.

Whether it's spending time in prayer, standing firm in your integrity at work, or leading your family with love and wisdom, your daily choices are shaping the man you are becoming. Every action and every decision is an opportunity to reflect God's design for your life. This week, we'll dive deeper into what it means to have a daily commitment to God's will. We'll examine how ordinary moments can become extraordinary when lived with intentionality and faithfulness.

Ask yourself: What areas of my daily life need to be more aligned with God's purpose? How can I better prioritize my relationship with Him and be more intentional in following His design? As we study together, be open to allowing God to shape your everyday routines into acts of worship and obedience, so that your life reflects His purpose in every detail.

- **Focus:** Living out God's design for manhood in every aspect of life.
- **Key Scriptures:** Genesis 1:26-28, 1 Corinthians 16:13-14

> *"Be on the alert, stand firm in the faith, act like men, be strong. Let all that you do be done in love."*

- Discussion Questions:

1. How has your understanding of biblical manhood changed over these four weeks?

2. What does it look like to live out biblical manhood in your family, workplace, and community?

3. What are areas your brother can help/ teach you to become a better man? A better Christian man?

- **Action Step:** Memorize 1 Corinthians 16:13-14 as a guiding principle for your life. Reflect on how you can apply this scripture in practical ways each day.

- **Man Up Challenge:** As you finish this study, write a personal prayer committing to live as a man who honors God's design. Share your commitment with a trusted brother in Christ for accountability.

### Ongoing Application:

- **Daily Discipline:** Continue daily Bible reading, prayer, and scripture memorization to reinforce the foundations of biblical manhood.
- **Accountability:** Find a brother in Christ to regularly discuss your progress and challenges as you seek to live out biblical manhood.

**Week 4 Bible Reading**: *Genesis 37–50; Matthew 11–13*

## Week 4- Using the 22 Questions for Accountability

John Wesley and his Holy Club were renowned for their dedication to spiritual growth and rigorous accountability. At the heart of their gatherings were 22 questions that challenged each member to examine their faith, actions, and intentions. These questions were designed to help men remain focused on their walk with Christ, to grow in holiness, and to hold each other accountable to living out the Gospel daily.

In a world full of distractions and temptations, it's easy to drift in our spiritual lives without even realizing it. The 22 questions serve as a powerful tool to bring us back into alignment with God's will and to cultivate a life of intentional faith. They cover areas such as integrity, personal holiness, and commitment to spiritual disciplines, calling us to examine our hearts deeply and honestly.

Using these questions for accountability, whether in a group setting or personal reflection, can strengthen your walk with Christ by fostering humility, transparency, and a commitment to spiritual growth. As we go through these questions, consider how they apply to your life and how you can use them to grow as a man of God. True accountability isn't just about pointing out faults; it's about walking alongside one another, encouraging one another, and pushing one another toward holiness.

In your final week for this session, we encourage you to reflect on these questions with a trusted brother in Christ. Reflect and review the past four weeks and check your **prayer request** and the people you are praying for. Did you see God move? Allow these questions to challenge you to greater faithfulness, as they have for countless men of faith through the centuries.

1. Am I consciously or unconsciously creating the impression that I am better than I really am? In other words, am I a hypocrite?
2. Am I honest in all my acts and words, or do I exaggerate?
3. Do I confidentially pass on to another what was told to me in confidence?
4. Can I be trusted?
5. Am I a slave to dress, friends, work, or habits?
6. Am I self-conscious, self-pitying, or self-justifying?
7. Did the Bible live in me today?

8. Do I give it time to speak to me everyday?
9. Am I enjoying prayer?
10. When did I last speak to someone else about my faith?
11. Do I pray about the money I spend?
12. Do I get to bed on time and get up on time?
13. Do I disobey God in anything?
14. Do I insist upon doing something about which my conscience is uneasy?
15. Am I defeated in any part of my life?
16. Am I jealous, impure, critical, irritable, touchy, or distrustful?
17. How do I spend my spare time?
18. Am I proud?
19. Do I thank God that I am not as other people, especially as the Pharisees who despised the publican?
20. Is there anyone whom I fear, dislike, disown, criticize, hold a resentment toward or disregard? If so, what am I doing about it?
21. Do I grumble or complain constantly?
22. Is Christ real to me?

*"Daily commitment to God's design means surrendering your plans to His purpose, trusting that His way is always better, and walking in obedience no matter the cost."*— **Charles Stanley**

# CHAPTER 2
# IDENTITY IN CHRIST

# IDENTITY IN CHRIST

## WEEK 5: A NEW CREATION IN CHRIST

When we come to faith in Christ, something miraculous happens, we are made new. The Bible tells us that in Christ, the old has passed away, and the new has come (2 Corinthians 5:17). This transformation is not just about a change in behavior; it's about a complete shift in our identity. We are no longer defined by our past mistakes, failures, or sins—we are defined by who we are in Christ.

This week, we will explore what it means to be a new creation in Christ. This identity is foundational to your journey as a godly man. It means that you are not bound by the old patterns of this world, but you are now empowered to live out a new life that reflects the character of Christ. As you go through this study, reflect on how this new identity changes everything—how you see yourself, how you relate to others, and how you live out your purpose.

God has called you to live differently because you have been made new. Your thoughts, actions, and priorities are now shaped by His Spirit living in you. This week, take time to embrace the reality of your new identity, letting go of anything from your past that tries to pull you back. You are no longer who you were; you are now a new creation, set apart for God's purposes.

- **Focus:** Understanding what it means to be a new creation in Christ.
- **Key Scripture:** 2 Corinthians 5:17

> *"17 Therefore if anyone is in Christ, he is a new creature; the old things passed away; behold, new things have come. "*

- Discussion Questions:

1. What does it mean to be a new creation in Christ?

_______________________________________________

_______________________________________________

_______________________________________________

_______________________________________________

_______________________________________________

2. How does this new identity change the way we view ourselves and others?

_______________________________________________

_______________________________________________

_______________________________________________

_______________________________________________

_______________________________________________

3. What are some things you want to change about your identity?

_______________________________________________

_______________________________________________

_______________________________________________

_______________________________________________

_______________________________________________

_______________________________________________

- **Action Step:** Reflect on the areas in your life where the "old self" is still present. Identify one area where you need to embrace your new identity in Christ.

- **Man Up Challenge:** Start each day this week by declaring your identity as a new creation in Christ. Write down one way you will live out this new identity in your daily life.

**Week 5 Bible Reading**: *Exodus 1–15; Matthew 14–16*

**Week 5 Accountability Questions for You and/ or Your Group: (End each week, holding each other accountable with these questions. Be honest, this is where we grow.)**

| | | Yes | No |
|---|---|---|---|
| 1. | Have you spent daily time in the Scriptures and in prayer? | | |
| 2. | Have you had any impure thoughts that would not glorify God? | | |
| 3. | Have you been completely above reproach in your financial dealings? | | |
| 4. | Have you spent quality relationship time with family and friends? | | |
| 5. | Have you done your 100% best in your job, school, home, etc.? | | |
| 6. | Have you told any half-truths or outright lies, putting yourself in a better light to those around you? | | |
| 7. | Have you shared the Gospel with an unbeliever this week? | | |
| 8. | Have you taken care of your body through daily physical exercise and proper eating/sleeping habits? | | |
| 9. | Have you allowed any person or circumstance to rob you of your joy? | | |
| 10. | Have you lied on any of your answers today? | | |

**Prayer Request**

- ____________________
- ____________________
- ____________________
- ____________________
- ____________________
- ____________________
- ____________________

**Name 5 People To Pray for this Week**

- ____________________
- ____________________
- ____________________
- ____________________
- ____________________
- ____________________
- ____________________

Each week, we will give you men in the Bible who exemplified the main theme. Take time this week to study these men.

**1. Paul – Identity Transformed from Persecutor to Apostle**

- Scripture: Galatians 2:20
  *"I have been crucified with Christ; and it is no longer I who live, but Christ lives in me; and the life which I now live in the flesh I live by faith in the Son of God, who loved me and gave Himself up for me."*
- Overview: Paul's identity was radically transformed after his encounter with Christ on the road to Damascus. From being a persecutor of Christians to becoming one of the most influential apostles, Paul embraced his new identity in Christ. His life and ministry were completely shaped by his faith in Jesus, as he recognized that his old self had been crucified and his new life was rooted in Christ alone.

**2. Peter – Identity Restored and Recommissioned by Christ**

- Scripture: 1 Peter 2:9
  *"But you are a chosen race, a royal priesthood, a holy nation, a people for God's own possession, so that you may proclaim the excellencies of Him who has called you out of darkness into His marvelous light."*
- Overview: Peter is a powerful example of a man whose identity was restored in Christ after failure. After denying Jesus three times, Peter was recommissioned by Jesus after the resurrection. Christ saw Peter not through the lens of his failures, but through his potential and the calling that God had placed on his life. Peter went on to be a leader in the early church, helping others embrace their new identity in Christ.

3. **John the Baptist – Identity as a Humble Forerunner for Christ**

- Scripture: John 3:30
  *"He must increase, but I must decrease."*
- Overview: John the Baptist knew his identity and purpose clearly: he was not the Messiah, but the one sent to prepare the way for Christ. His life was marked by humility and devotion to his calling, always pointing others to Jesus. John's understanding of his identity in God's plan gave him the boldness to preach repentance and call people to prepare for the coming of the Savior.

*"Your identity in Christ defines everything about you. It's not about who the world says you are or who you used to be—it's about who God says you are now. Embrace that identity, and let it shape the way you live, lead, and serve."*

**— Jody Burkeen**

# CRUCIFIED WITH CHRIST

## WEEK 6: CRUCIFIED WITH CHRIST

One of the most profound truths of the Christian life is that when we come to Christ, we are not only made new, but our old self is crucified with Him. Galatians 2:20 says, *"I have been crucified with Christ; it is no longer I who live, but Christ lives in me."* This means that our former way of life—dominated by sin, selfishness, and worldly desires—has been put to death, and we now live through the power and presence of Christ within us.

This week, we will explore what it means to be crucified with Christ. This isn't just a metaphor or a theological concept; it's a radical transformation that calls us to die to our old ways and live a life that is fully surrendered to Christ. Being crucified with Christ means that we no longer live for ourselves, but for Him who gave Himself for us. It's a daily choice to deny our flesh, take up our cross, and follow Him.

As you go through this study, reflect on the areas of your life where the old self still tries to take control. What habits, attitudes, or desires need to be crucified? In what ways can you allow Christ to live more fully in you? This week is about embracing the freedom and new life that comes from dying to self and living for Christ. Remember, the same power that raised Jesus from the dead is now at work in you, enabling you to live a life of victory and purpose.

- **Focus:** Understanding the significance of being crucified with Christ.
- **Key Scripture:** Galatians 2:20

> *"[20] I have been crucified with Christ; and it is no longer I who live, but Christ lives in me; and the life which I now live in the flesh I live by faith in the Son of God, who loved me and gave Himself up for me."*

- **Discussion Questions:**

1. What does it mean to be crucified with Christ?

_______________________________________________

_______________________________________________

_______________________________________________

_______________________________________________

_______________________________________________

_______________________________________________

_______________________________________________

_______________________________________________

2. How does this truth affect how we should live our daily lives as men of God?

_______________________________________________

_______________________________________________

_______________________________________________

_______________________________________________

_______________________________________________

_______________________________________________

_______________________________________________

_______________________________________________

- **Action Step:** Consider areas where you are still living according to the "flesh" rather than by faith in Christ. Surrender one of these areas to God this week

- **Man Up Challenge:** Each day, intentionally die to one desire or habit that is not aligned with Christ. Replace it with a Christ-centered action. Write your desires down that you are willing to lose.

**Week 6 Bible Reading**: *Exodus 16–31; Matthew 17–19*

**Week 6 Accountability Questions for You and/ or Your Group: (End each week, holding each other accountable with these questions. Be honest, this is where we grow.)**

| | | Yes | No |
|---|---|---|---|
| 1. | Have you spent daily time in the Scriptures and in prayer? | | |
| 2. | Have you had any impure thoughts that would not glorify God? | | |
| 3. | Have you been completely above reproach in your financial dealings? | | |
| 4. | Have you spent quality relationship time with family and friends? | | |
| 5. | Have you done your 100% best in your job, school, home, etc.? | | |
| 6. | Have you told any half-truths or outright lies, putting yourself in a better light to those around you? | | |
| 7. | Have you shared the Gospel with an unbeliever this week? | | |
| 8. | Have you taken care of your body through daily physical exercise and proper eating/sleeping habits? | | |
| 9. | Have you allowed any person or circumstance to rob you of your joy? | | |
| 10. | Have you lied on any of your answers today? | | |

**Prayer Request**

- ______________________
- ______________________
- ______________________
- ______________________
- ______________________
- ______________________
- ______________________

**Name 5 People To Pray for this Week**

- ______________________
- ______________________
- ______________________
- ______________________
- ______________________
- ______________________
- ______________________

**Each week, we will give you men in the Bible who exemplified the main theme. Take time this week to study these men.**

**1. John the Apostle – Living a Life of Surrender and Love for Christ**

- Scripture: 1 John 3:16
  *"We know love by this, that He laid down His life for us; and we ought to lay down our lives for the brethren."*

- Overview: John, known as the "disciple whom Jesus loved," lived a life dedicated to Christ after witnessing His crucifixion and resurrection. John's teachings reflect a life fully surrendered to Christ, especially in his writings about love and sacrifice. John understood that being crucified with Christ meant laying down one's life for others, living in total devotion to Christ, and reflecting His love in all things.

**2. Timothy – Crucified with Christ through Faithful Ministry**

- Scripture: 2 Timothy 1:8
  "Therefore do not be ashamed of the testimony of our Lord or of me His prisoner, but join with me in suffering for the gospel according to the power of God."

- Overview: Timothy was mentored by Paul and lived a life of commitment and sacrifice for the sake of the Gospel. While not physically crucified, Timothy exemplified being "crucified with Christ" by embracing a life of ministry that often required suffering, self-denial, and unwavering dedication. His willingness to endure hardships for the sake of Christ and the church shows a man fully surrendered to God's will.

**3. James – Leading the Jerusalem Church with Humility and Sacrifice**

- Scripture: James 1:2-3
  "Consider it all joy, my brethren, when you encounter various trials, knowing that the testing of your faith produces endurance."

- Overview: James, the brother of Jesus, became a key leader in the early church in Jerusalem. His leadership, characterized by humility and perseverance through persecution, reflects a man who was crucified with Christ. James' epistle emphasizes the need to endure trials and live a life of active faith, trusting in Christ through suffering and sacrifice. His life and leadership showed that being crucified with Christ means living with steadfastness and faith under pressure.

> *"The call to follow Christ is the call to die—to die to self, to die to sin, to die to the world. Only when we are crucified with Christ can we truly live in the freedom and power of His resurrection."* — **John Stott**

# LIVING BY FAITH, NOT BY FLESH

## WEEK 7: LIVING BY FAITH, NOT BY FLESH

As followers of Christ, we are called to live a life that is led by faith, not by the desires of the flesh. The Bible reminds us that the flesh, with its sinful nature and worldly cravings, is constantly at war with the Spirit. Living by the flesh leads to destruction, but living by faith leads to life and peace in Christ.

The apostle Paul teaches us in Galatians 5:16-17, *"But I say, walk by the Spirit, and you will not carry out the desire of the flesh. For the flesh sets its desire against the Spirit, and the Spirit against the flesh; for these are in opposition to one another, so that you may not do the things that you please."* This battle between the flesh and the Spirit is something we face daily, but God gives us the strength to live victoriously through faith.

Living by faith means surrendering control of our lives to Christ and trusting Him to guide us, even when our flesh wants to take the easy way out or satisfy worldly desires. It requires daily dependence on the Holy Spirit, listening to His promptings, and choosing obedience over the fleeting pleasures of sin. Faith compels us to live in alignment with God's Word, while the flesh pulls us toward selfishness, pride, and sin.

This week, we will explore what it means to truly live by faith. You will be challenged to examine areas of your life where the flesh still has control and to commit to walking in the Spirit. Ask yourself: Am I living according to the Spirit, or am I letting the desires of my flesh dictate my actions and decisions? Remember, God has given you the power to overcome the flesh through His Spirit and to walk in faith, trusting Him every step of the way.

- Focus: Living a life of faith, grounded in Christ's identity.
- Key Scripture: Galatians 2:20

> *"I have been crucified with Christ; and it is no longer I who live, but Christ lives in me; and the life which I now live in the flesh I live by faith in the Son of God, who loved me and gave Himself up for me."*

- Discussion Questions:

1. What does it mean to live by faith in the Son of God?

2. How does faith shape the way we approach challenges, relationships, and responsibilities?

- Action Step: Identify one area of your life where you need to trust Christ more fully. Take a specific step of faith in this area this week.

- Man Up Challenge: This week, practice living by faith in a tangible way. Whether it's in your family, work, or personal life, choose one specific area where you will lean into faith rather than your own strength.

**Week 7 Bible Reading**: *Exodus 32–40; Matthew 20–22*

**Week 7 Accountability Questions for You and/ or Your Group: (End each week, holding each other accountable with these questions. Be honest, this is where we grow.)**

| | | Yes | No |
|---|---|---|---|
| 1. | Have you spent daily time in the Scriptures and in prayer? | | |
| 2. | Have you had any impure thoughts that would not glorify God? | | |
| 3. | Have you been completely above reproach in your financial dealings? | | |
| 4. | Have you spent quality relationship time with family and friends? | | |
| 5. | Have you done your 100% best in your job, school, home, etc.? | | |
| 6. | Have you told any half-truths or outright lies, putting yourself in a better light to those around you? | | |
| 7. | Have you shared the Gospel with an unbeliever this week? | | |
| 8. | Have you taken care of your body through daily physical exercise and proper eating/sleeping habits? | | |
| 9. | Have you allowed any person or circumstance to rob you of your joy? | | |
| 10. | Have you lied on any of your answers today? | | |

| **Prayer Request** | **Name 5 People To Pray for this Week** |
|---|---|
| • ______________________ | • ______________________ |
| • ______________________ | • ______________________ |
| • ______________________ | • ______________________ |
| • ______________________ | • ______________________ |
| • ______________________ | • ______________________ |
| • ______________________ | • ______________________ |
| • ______________________ | • ______________________ |

**Each week, we will give you men in the Bible who exemplified the main theme. Take time this week to study these men.**

**1. Abraham – Living by Faith in God's Promises**

- Scripture: Hebrews 11:8-10
  "By faith Abraham, when he was called, obeyed by going out to a place which he was to receive for an inheritance; and he went out, not knowing where he was going. By faith he lived as an alien in the land of promise, as in a foreign land, dwelling in tents with Isaac and Jacob, fellow heirs of the same promise; for he was looking for the city which has foundations, whose architect and builder is God."

- Overview: Abraham's life is a powerful example of living by faith, not by sight or fleshly security. He left his home and all that he knew, trusting in God's promise of a new land and a future nation. His obedience to God, even when he didn't know the full picture, showed a deep faith in God's plan, over his personal desires or fears.

**2. Moses – Choosing Faith Over the Pleasures of Egypt**

- Scripture: Hebrews 11:24-26
  "By faith Moses, when he had grown up, refused to be called the son of Pharaoh's daughter, choosing rather to endure ill-treatment with the people of God than to enjoy the passing pleasures of sin, considering the reproach of Christ greater riches than the treasures of Egypt; for he was looking to the reward."

- Overview: Moses rejected the fleeting pleasures and treasures of Egypt, choosing instead to live by faith and identify with the people of God. He could have pursued a life of wealth, power, and comfort in Pharaoh's household, but he chose to follow God's call, enduring hardship for the sake of the greater spiritual reward.

**3. Joseph – Faith in God's Plan Amid Trials**

- Scripture: Genesis 50:20
  "As for you, you meant evil against me, but God meant it for good in order to bring about this present result, to preserve many people alive."

- Overview: Joseph exemplified living by faith throughout his life, even when faced with betrayal, slavery, and imprisonment. Rather than giving in to bitterness, anger, or revenge, Joseph trusted in God's sovereign plan. He believed that God was working through his hardships for a greater purpose, and he faithfully lived out that belief, even in the most difficult circumstances.

> *"Living by faith means trusting God even when your flesh screams for control. It's choosing obedience over comfort, surrender over selfishness, and God's will over your own desires."*— **Jody Burkeen**

# EMBRACING YOUR IDENTITY IN CHRIST

## WEEK 8: EMBRACING YOUR IDENTITY IN CHRIST

One of the most powerful and life-changing truths in Scripture is that when you come to faith in Christ, your identity is forever transformed. You are no longer defined by your past mistakes, failures, or the labels the world puts on you. Instead, you are a new creation, fully loved and accepted by God, set apart for His purposes. Embracing your identity in Christ means understanding who you are according to God's Word and living out that truth daily.

The Bible tells us in 2 Corinthians 5:17 , *"Therefore if anyone is in Christ, he is a new creature; the old things passed away; behold, new things have come."* This verse reminds us that our old life—the life defined by sin and separation from God—has been put to death, and we are now spiritually alive in Christ. But living in this new identity requires intentionality and faith. It's easy to fall back into old patterns of thinking or allow the world's opinions to shape how we see ourselves. However, when you fully embrace who you are in Christ, it changes how you view your purpose, relationships, and daily decisions.

This week, we'll explore what it means to embrace your identity in Christ and reject the lies that try to pull you back into the old self. You'll be challenged to see yourself as God sees you—righteous, redeemed, and empowered by the Holy Spirit. Ask yourself: Am I living according to my true identity in Christ, or am I allowing the world and my past to define me? It's time to embrace the truth of who you are in Him and live boldly and confidently as a new creation.

- Focus: Understanding the full impact of your identity in Christ and living it out boldly.
- Key Scripture: 2 Corinthians 5:17, Galatians 2:20

> *"Therefore if anyone is in Christ, he is a new creature; the old things passed away; behold, new things have come."*

- Discussion Questions:

1. How has your understanding of your identity in Christ changed over these four weeks?

2. How does your new identity affect your role as a man, husband, father, or leader?

- Action Step: Write down a personal mission statement based on your identity in Christ. How will this mission guide your daily life, decisions, and relationships? See my personal mission statement on pg.___

- Man Up Challenge: Share your mission statement with a trusted friend or brother in Christ. Ask them to hold you accountable to live out your identity in Christ.

## Ongoing Application:

- Daily Discipline: Continue reflecting on your identity in Christ through daily prayer, scripture reading, and faith-driven action.
- Accountability: Partner with a fellow believer to encourage and challenge one another to live out your new identity.

**Week 8 Bible Reading**: *Leviticus 1–16; Matthew 23–25*

## Week 8- Using the 22 Questions for Accountability

John Wesley and his Holy Club were renowned for their dedication to spiritual growth and rigorous accountability. At the heart of their gatherings were 22 questions that challenged each member to examine their faith, actions, and intentions. These questions were designed to help men remain focused on their walk with Christ, to grow in holiness, and to hold each other accountable to living out the Gospel daily.

In a world full of distractions and temptations, it's easy to drift in our spiritual lives without even realizing it. The 22 questions serve as a powerful tool to bring us back into alignment with God's will and to cultivate a life of intentional faith. They cover areas such as integrity, personal holiness, and commitment to spiritual disciplines, calling us to examine our hearts deeply and honestly.

Using these questions for accountability, whether in a group setting or personal reflection, can strengthen your walk with Christ by fostering humility, transparency, and a commitment to spiritual growth. As we go through these questions, consider how they apply to your life and how you can use them to grow as a man of God. True accountability isn't just about pointing out faults; it's about walking alongside one another, encouraging one another, and pushing one another toward holiness.

In your final week for this session, we encourage you to reflect on these questions with a trusted brother in Christ. Reflect and review the past four weeks and check your **prayer request** and the people you are praying for. Did you see God move? Allow these questions to challenge you to greater faithfulness, as they have for countless men of faith through the centuries.

1. Am I consciously or unconsciously creating the impression that I am better than I really am? In other words, am I a hypocrite?
2. Am I honest in all my acts and words, or do I exaggerate?
3. Do I confidentially pass on to another what was told to me in confidence?
4. Can I be trusted?
5. Am I a slave to dress, friends, work, or habits?
6. Am I self-conscious, self-pitying, or self-justifying?
7. Did the Bible live in me today?

8. Do I give it time to speak to me everyday?
9. Am I enjoying prayer?
10. When did I last speak to someone else about my faith?
11. Do I pray about the money I spend?
12. Do I get to bed on time and get up on time?
13. Do I disobey God in anything?
14. Do I insist upon doing something about which my conscience is uneasy?
15. Am I defeated in any part of my life?
16. Am I jealous, impure, critical, irritable, touchy, or distrustful?
17. How do I spend my spare time?
18. Am I proud?
19. Do I thank God that I am not as other people, especially as the Pharisees who despised the publican?
20. Is there anyone whom I fear, dislike, disown, criticize, hold a resentment toward or disregard? If so, what am I doing about it?
21. Do I grumble or complain constantly?
22. Is Christ real to me?

> *"When you embrace your identity in Christ, you no longer live for the approval of others but rest in the truth that you are fully known and fully loved by God."*— **Tim Keller**

# CHAPTER 3
# SPIRITUAL DISCIPLINE

# TRAINING FOR GODLINESS

## WEEK 9: TRAINING FOR GODLINESS

Just like physical training strengthens the body, spiritual training is essential for developing godliness and growing in your relationship with Christ. The Bible compares the pursuit of godliness to the discipline and perseverance of an athlete. In 1 Timothy 4:7-8, Paul writes, *"Discipline yourself for the purpose of godliness; for bodily discipline is only of little profit, but godliness is profitable for all things, since it holds promise for the present life and also for the life to come."* Training for godliness doesn't happen by accident; it requires intentionality, discipline, and a daily commitment to spiritual growth.

Godliness is not just about avoiding sin or following rules—it's about becoming more like Christ in every aspect of your life. This training involves spending time in God's Word, praying consistently, repenting of sin, and allowing the Holy Spirit to transform your heart and mind. As you train, you grow in wisdom, strength, and the ability to live out your faith in a way that impacts others.

This week, we'll explore what it means to train for godliness and why it's a lifelong pursuit. Just as physical training requires effort and endurance, so does growing in spiritual maturity. The more you train yourself in godliness, the more you'll experience the abundant life God has promised and be equipped to fulfill the purpose He has for you. Ask yourself: What spiritual disciplines am I actively training in, and how can I become more intentional in my pursuit of godliness?

- Focus: Understanding the importance of spiritual discipline.
- Key Scripture: 1 Timothy 4:7-8

> *"But have nothing to do with worldly fables fit only for old women. On the other hand, discipline yourself for the purpose of godliness; for bodily discipline is only of little profit, but godliness is profitable for all things, since it holds promise for the present life and also for the life to come."*

- Discussion Questions:

1. How is spiritual discipline like physical training?

2. What are the benefits of godliness, both in this life and the life to come?

- Action Step: Reflect on your current spiritual habits. Identify one area where you need to grow in spiritual discipline (prayer, Bible reading, worship, etc.).

- Man Up Challenge: Start a daily routine this week focused on a specific spiritual habit you want to develop. Begin each day with prayer and meditation on 1 Timothy 4:7

**Week 9 Bible Reading**: *Leviticus 17–27; Matthew 26–28*

**Week 9 Accountability Questions for You and/ or Your Group:** (End each week, holding each other accountable with these questions. Be honest, this is where we grow.)

| | | Yes | No |
|---|---|---|---|
| 1. | Have you spent daily time in the Scriptures and in prayer? | | |
| 2. | Have you had any impure thoughts that would not glorify God? | | |
| 3. | Have you been completely above reproach in your financial dealings? | | |
| 4. | Have you spent quality relationship time with family and friends? | | |
| 5. | Have you done your 100% best in your job, school, home, etc.? | | |
| 6. | Have you told any half-truths or outright lies, putting yourself in a better light to those around you? | | |
| 7. | Have you shared the Gospel with an unbeliever this week? | | |
| 8. | Have you taken care of your body through daily physical exercise and proper eating/sleeping habits? | | |
| 9. | Have you allowed any person or circumstance to rob you of your joy? | | |
| 10. | Have you lied on any of your answers today? | | |

**Prayer Request**

- ____________________
- ____________________
- ____________________
- ____________________
- ____________________
- ____________________
- ____________________

**Name 5 People To Pray for this Week**

- ____________________
- ____________________
- ____________________
- ____________________
- ____________________
- ____________________
- ____________________

Each week, we will give you men in the Bible who exemplified the main theme. Take time this week to study these men.

**1. Paul – Disciplined for the Sake of the Gospel**

- Scripture: 1 Corinthians 9:25-27
  "Everyone who competes in the games exercises self-control in all things. They then do it to receive a perishable wreath, but we an imperishable. Therefore I run in such a way, as not without aim; I box in such a way, as not beating the air; but I discipline my body and make it my slave, so that, after I have preached to others, I myself will not be disqualified."

- Overview: Paul often used the metaphor of an athlete training for competition to describe the pursuit of godliness. His life was a testament to spiritual discipline, as he endured hardships, committed to prayer, studied God's Word, and continually sought to grow in his relationship with Christ. Paul's focus on discipline shows us that spiritual growth requires ongoing effort and self-control.

**2. Daniel – A Life of Consistent Prayer and Devotion**

- Scripture: Daniel 6:10
  "Now when Daniel knew that the document was signed, he entered his house (now in his roof chamber he had windows open toward Jerusalem); and he continued kneeling on his knees three times a day, praying and giving thanks before his God, as he had been doing previously."

- Overview: Daniel exemplified training for godliness through his consistent prayer life and devotion to God, even in the face of opposition. Despite living in a foreign land with different customs and facing threats to his life, Daniel's disciplined spiritual practices, such as daily prayer and reliance on God, shaped his godly character and gave him strength to stand firm in his faith.

**3. Timothy – A Man Trained by Scripture and Discipleship**

- Scripture: 1 Timothy 4:7-8
  "But have nothing to do with worldly fables fit only for old women. On the other hand, discipline yourself for the purpose of godliness; for bodily discipline is only of little profit, but godliness is profitable for all things, since it holds promise for the present life and also for the life to come."

- Overview: Timothy was a young leader who was trained in godliness through the teachings of Scripture and mentorship from Paul. He was instructed to devote himself to the spiritual disciplines necessary for godly leadership, emphasizing the importance of growing in faith and understanding God's Word. His life was a reflection of someone who took spiritual training seriously in order to be effective in ministry.

*Callout- "Training for godliness doesn't happen overnight. It's the daily discipline of surrendering to God's will, investing in His Word, and allowing the Holy Spirit to shape you into the man He has called you to be."* — **Jody Burkeen**

# SHARPENING ONE ANOTHER

## WEEK 10: SHARPENING ONE ANOTHER

In the Christian life, we are not called to walk alone. God has designed us to grow in faith, wisdom, and godliness through relationships with other believers. Proverbs 27:17 tells us, *"Iron sharpens iron, so one man sharpens another."* Just as iron tools need sharpening to be effective, we too need other men in our lives to challenge, encourage, and hold us accountable. This process of sharpening one another is how we grow stronger, wiser, and more effective in living out our faith.

Sharpening one another isn't always easy. It requires vulnerability, humility, and a willingness to be both corrected and encouraged by others. But it is through these relationships that God molds us into the men He has called us to be. When we surround ourselves with godly men who push us to live in accordance with God's Word, we are equipped to face life's challenges and fulfill our purpose in His Kingdom.

This week, we will explore what it means to truly sharpen one another in the faith. We'll look at the importance of accountability, the power of encouragement, and the role of godly friendships in our spiritual growth. As you reflect on your relationships, ask yourself: Who in my life is sharpening me, and how am I sharpening others? Together, we can grow stronger and more faithful as we pursue godliness side by side.

- Focus: The role of community and accountability in spiritual growth.
- Key Scripture: Proverbs 27:17

> *" Iron sharpens iron, So one man sharpens another."*

- Discussion Questions:

1. Why is it important to have accountability in our spiritual lives?

2. How can relationships with other godly men sharpen your faith?

- Action Step: Identify someone who can hold you accountable in your spiritual walk. Set up a time to regularly meet for prayer and study.

- Man Up Challenge: Choose an accountability partner this week and commit to weekly check-ins for encouragement, prayer, and mutual spiritual sharpening.

**Week 10 Bible Reading**: *Numbers 1–15; Mark 1–3*

**Week 10 Accountability Questions for You and/ or Your Group: (End each week, holding each other accountable with these questions. Be honest, this is where we grow.)**

| | | Yes | No |
|---|---|---|---|
| 1. | Have you spent daily time in the Scriptures and in prayer? | | |
| 2. | Have you had any impure thoughts that would not glorify God? | | |
| 3. | Have you been completely above reproach in your financial dealings? | | |
| 4. | Have you spent quality relationship time with family and friends? | | |
| 5. | Have you done your 100% best in your job, school, home, etc.? | | |
| 6. | Have you told any half-truths or outright lies, putting yourself in a better light to those around you? | | |
| 7. | Have you shared the Gospel with an unbeliever this week? | | |
| 8. | Have you taken care of your body through daily physical exercise and proper eating/sleeping habits? | | |
| 9. | Have you allowed any person or circumstance to rob you of your joy? | | |
| 10. | Have you lied on any of your answers today? | | |

| **Prayer Request** | **Name 5 People To Pray for this Week** |
|---|---|
| • ______________ | • ______________ |
| • ______________ | • ______________ |
| • ______________ | • ______________ |
| • ______________ | • ______________ |
| • ______________ | • ______________ |
| • ______________ | • ______________ |
| • ______________ | • ______________ |

Each week, we will give you men in the Bible who exemplified the main theme. Take time this week to study these men.

**1. David and Jonathan – A Friendship of Mutual Strengthening**

- Scripture: 1 Samuel 23:16-17
  "And Jonathan, Saul's son, arose and went to David at Horesh, and encouraged him in God. Thus he said to him, 'Do not be afraid, because the hand of Saul my father will not find you, and you will be king over Israel and I will be next to you; and Saul my father knows that also.'"

- Overview: Jonathan and David shared a deep friendship rooted in loyalty, faith, and mutual encouragement. Jonathan continually strengthened David's faith, even in times of great danger, helping David trust in God's plan for his life. This friendship was marked by a commitment to sharpening one another spiritually.

**2. Paul and Timothy – Discipleship and Accountability**

- Scripture: 2 Timothy 2:2
  "The things which you have heard from me in the presence of many witnesses, entrust these to faithful men who will be able to teach others also."

- Overview: Paul mentored and discipled Timothy, teaching him how to lead the church and stand firm in his faith. Through this relationship, Paul sharpened Timothy's spiritual understanding and leadership skills, encouraging him to pass on what he had learned to others. Their bond was one of accountability and mutual growth in the faith.

**3. Moses and Aaron – Strengthening One Another in Leadership**

- Scripture: Exodus 4:14-16
  "Then the anger of the Lord burned against Moses, and He said, 'Is there not your brother Aaron the Levite? I know that he speaks fluently. And moreover, behold, he is coming out to meet you; when he sees you, he will be glad in his heart. You are to speak to him and put the words in his mouth; and I, even I, will be with your mouth and his mouth, and I will teach you what you are to do.'"

- Overview: God called Moses to lead His people, but Moses struggled with feelings of inadequacy. Aaron, his brother, was provided by God to speak on Moses' behalf and help him in his mission. Together, they sharpened one another's leadership abilities, strengthening each other as they carried out God's plan.

> *"True friendship in Christ means that we sharpen each other—challenging one another to be more like Christ, to reject sin, and to pursue godliness. We are called to be iron sharpening iron, not leaving each other unchanged, but growing together in faith."*— **John Piper**

# THE DISCIPLINE OF PRAYER

## WEEK 11: THE DISCIPLINE OF PRAYER

Prayer is one of the most powerful and essential disciplines in the life of a believer. It is our direct line of communication with God, where we bring our praises, confessions, requests, and thanksgiving before Him. Yet, it is more than just speaking to God—it's a time of listening and aligning our hearts with His will. Prayer is not a passive activity; it requires discipline, intentionality, and consistency to cultivate a meaningful and transformative relationship with God.

The Bible consistently emphasizes the importance of prayer. Jesus Himself modeled a life of prayer, often withdrawing to pray, even during the busiest moments of His ministry. In Philippians 4:6, we are told, *"Be anxious for nothing, but in everything by prayer and supplication with thanksgiving let your requests be made known to God."* Prayer is not just for times of crisis, but it is to be an ongoing part of our daily lives—our source of strength, guidance, and peace.

This week, we will explore the discipline of prayer, looking at what it means to cultivate a consistent prayer life. Prayer is not about perfect words or rituals, but about a sincere heart seeking after God. As you reflect on your own prayer life, consider how you can grow in this discipline. Are you setting aside time to pray daily? Are you seeking God's will in your prayers, or simply presenting your requests? The discipline of prayer will draw you closer to God and strengthen your faith, helping you live out His purpose with clarity and confidence.

- Focus: Developing a consistent prayer life.
- Key Scripture: Philippians 4:6

> *" Be anxious for nothing, but in everything by prayer and supplication with thanksgiving let your requests be made known to God."*

- Discussion Questions:

1. Why is prayer essential in our spiritual discipline?

2. How can we cultivate a deeper and more consistent prayer life?

- Action Step: Create a daily prayer schedule, including a time of thanksgiving, confession, and intercession. Set aside a specific time each day for uninterrupted prayer.

- Man Up Challenge: Pray with your accountability partner at least once this week. Be intentional about praying for their needs as well as your own.

**Week 11 Bible Reading**: *Numbers 16–36; Mark 4–6*

**Week 11 Accountability Questions for You and/ or Your Group: (End each week, holding each other accountable with these questions. Be honest, this is where we grow.)**

| | | Yes | No |
|---|---|---|---|
| 1. | Have you spent daily time in the Scriptures and in prayer? | | |
| 2. | Have you had any impure thoughts that would not glorify God? | | |
| 3. | Have you been completely above reproach in your financial dealings? | | |
| 4. | Have you spent quality relationship time with family and friends? | | |
| 5. | Have you done your 100% best in your job, school, home, etc.? | | |
| 6. | Have you told any half-truths or outright lies, putting yourself in a better light to those around you? | | |
| 7. | Have you shared the Gospel with an unbeliever this week? | | |
| 8. | Have you taken care of your body through daily physical exercise and proper eating/sleeping habits? | | |
| 9. | Have you allowed any person or circumstance to rob you of your joy? | | |
| 10. | Have you lied on any of your answers today? | | |

| Prayer Request | Name 5 People To Pray for this Week |
|---|---|
| • ______________________ | • ______________________ |
| • ______________________ | • ______________________ |
| • ______________________ | • ______________________ |
| • ______________________ | • ______________________ |
| • ______________________ | • ______________________ |
| • ______________________ | • ______________________ |
| • ______________________ | • ______________________ |

**Each week, we will give you men in the Bible who exemplified the main theme. Take time this week to study these men.**

**1. Daniel – Committed to Daily Prayer Despite Opposition**

- Scripture: Daniel 6:10
  "Now when Daniel knew that the document was signed, he entered his house (now in his roof chamber he had windows open toward Jerusalem); and he continued kneeling on his knees three times a day, praying and giving thanks before his God, as he had been doing previously."

- Overview: Daniel was known for his disciplined and consistent prayer life, even in the face of opposition. Despite the threat of death, Daniel continued to pray to God three times a day, showing his unwavering commitment to communication with God. His prayer discipline not only sustained him spiritually but also brought glory to God through his steadfast faith.

**2. David – A Heart After God Expressed Through Prayer**

- Scripture: Psalm 5:3
  "In the morning, O Lord, You will hear my voice; in the morning I will order my prayer to You and eagerly watch."

- Overview: David, known as a man after God's own heart, was a man of deep prayer. Many of the Psalms reflect David's heart of prayer, whether in times of praise, repentance, or pleading for God's help. His life exemplified a constant reliance on God, and prayer was his way of drawing near to the Lord in every situation.

**3. Jesus – A Life Centered on Prayer**

- Scripture: Luke 5:16
  "But Jesus Himself would often slip away to the wilderness and pray."

- Overview: Jesus, the ultimate example of godliness, frequently withdrew to pray. Even during His busiest ministry seasons, He made time to commune with the Father in solitude. His disciplined prayer life was central to His strength, guidance, and obedience to the Father's will. Jesus modeled the importance of prioritizing prayer, no matter the demands of life.

*Call out- "True friendship in Christ means that we sharpen each other—challenging one another to be more like Christ, to reject sin, and to pursue godliness. We are called to be iron sharpening iron, not leaving each other unchanged, but growing together in faith."* — **John Piper**

# BUILDING A SPIRITUAL ROUTINE

## WEEK 12: BUILDING A SPIRITUAL ROUTINE

In the same way that physical fitness requires a consistent workout plan, spiritual growth also demands discipline and intentionality. Building a spiritual routine is essential for cultivating a deeper relationship with God, developing godly habits, and staying focused on your walk with Christ. Just as an athlete trains daily to become stronger, we too must train ourselves spiritually to grow in faith, wisdom, and holiness.

A spiritual routine involves daily practices such as reading the Bible, prayer, worship, and reflection. These disciplines help you stay connected to God, guide your decisions, and equip you for life's challenges. In 1 Timothy 4:7-8, Paul writes, *"Discipline yourself for the purpose of godliness; for bodily discipline is only of little profit, but godliness is profitable for all things, since it holds promise for the present life and also for the life to come."* Developing a spiritual routine isn't about checking off a list of religious duties—it's about building habits that keep you close to God and help you grow in His likeness.

This week, we will explore how to create and maintain a spiritual routine that strengthens your faith and helps you stay grounded in God's Word. As you reflect on your daily habits, ask yourself: Am I intentionally setting aside time to invest in my relationship with God? How can I structure my day to ensure that spiritual disciplines are a priority? By building a consistent spiritual routine, you will be better equipped to live out your faith and fulfill God's calling on your life.

- Focus: Establishing a holistic spiritual routine that includes prayer, Bible study, and accountability.
- Key Scriptures: 1 Timothy 4:7-8, Proverbs 27:17

> *"But have nothing to do with worldly fables fit only for old women. On the other hand, discipline yourself for the purpose of godliness; for bodily discipline is only of little profit, but godliness is profitable for all things, since it holds promise for the present life and also for the life to come."*

- Discussion Questions:

1. How have your spiritual habits changed over the past month?

_______________________________________________

_______________________________________________

_______________________________________________

_______________________________________________

_______________________________________________

_______________________________________________

_______________________________________________

2. What is the impact of having a consistent spiritual routine in your relationship with God?

_______________________________________________

_______________________________________________

_______________________________________________

_______________________________________________

_______________________________________________

_______________________________________________

_______________________________________________

- Action Step: Finalize your daily spiritual routine. It should include time for prayer, Bible study, and weekly check-ins with your accountability partner.

___

___

___

___

___

___

___

- Man Up Challenge: Share your spiritual routine with your accountability partner and commit to keeping each other on track. Reflect on any changes you've seen in your life due to these spiritual disciplines.

___

___

___

___

___

___

___

### Ongoing Application:

- Daily Discipline: Continue practicing your spiritual routine daily, and seek to grow in new areas of spiritual discipline.
- Accountability: Keep meeting with your accountability partner regularly to ensure growth, encouragement, and ongoing support.

**Week 12 Bible Reading**: *Deuteronomy 1–15; Mark 7–8*

## Week 12- Using the 22 Questions for Accountability

John Wesley and his Holy Club were renowned for their dedication to spiritual growth and rigorous accountability. At the heart of their gatherings were 22 questions that challenged each member to examine their faith, actions, and intentions. These questions were designed to help men remain focused on their walk with Christ, to grow in holiness, and to hold each other accountable to living out the Gospel daily.

In a world full of distractions and temptations, it's easy to drift in our spiritual lives without even realizing it. The 22 questions serve as a powerful tool to bring us back into alignment with God's will and to cultivate a life of intentional faith. They cover areas such as integrity, personal holiness, and commitment to spiritual disciplines, calling us to examine our hearts deeply and honestly.

Using these questions for accountability, whether in a group setting or personal reflection, can strengthen your walk with Christ by fostering humility, transparency, and a commitment to spiritual growth. As we go through these questions, consider how they apply to your life and how you can use them to grow as a man of God. True accountability isn't just about pointing out faults; it's about walking alongside one another, encouraging one another, and pushing one another toward holiness.

In your final week for this session, we encourage you to reflect on these questions with a trusted brother in Christ. Reflect and review the past four weeks and check your **prayer request** and the people you are praying for. Did you see God move? Allow these questions to challenge you to greater faithfulness, as they have for countless men of faith through the centuries.

1. Am I consciously or unconsciously creating the impression that I am better than I really am? In other words, am I a hypocrite?
2. Am I honest in all my acts and words, or do I exaggerate?
3. Do I confidentially pass on to another what was told to me in confidence?
4. Can I be trusted?
5. Am I a slave to dress, friends, work, or habits?
6. Am I self-conscious, self-pitying, or self-justifying?
7. Did the Bible live in me today?

8. Do I give it time to speak to me everyday?
9. Am I enjoying prayer?
10. When did I last speak to someone else about my faith?
11. Do I pray about the money I spend?
12. Do I get to bed on time and get up on time?
13. Do I disobey God in anything?
14. Do I insist upon doing something about which my conscience is uneasy?
15. Am I defeated in any part of my life?
16. Am I jealous, impure, critical, irritable, touchy, or distrustful?
17. How do I spend my spare time?
18. Am I proud?
19. Do I thank God that I am not as other people, especially as the Pharisees who despised the publican?
20. Is there anyone whom I fear, dislike, disown, criticize, hold a resentment toward or disregard? If so, what am I doing about it?
21. Do I grumble or complain constantly?
22. Is Christ real to me?

> *"A spiritual routine isn't about checking boxes—it's about creating space daily to encounter God, hear His voice, and align your heart with His will."*— **John Piper**

# CHAPTER 4
# LEADERSHIP IN THE HOME

# LOVE AND SACRIFICE IN MARRIAGE

## WEEK 13: LOVE AND SACRIFICE IN MARRIAGE

Marriage is one of the most powerful and sacred relationships God designed, built on the foundation of love and sacrifice. In Ephesians 5:25, husbands are commanded to *"love your wives, just as Christ also loved the church and gave Himself up for her."* This love is not just a feeling but a deliberate choice to put your spouse's needs above your own, reflecting the selfless love that Christ showed for us through His sacrifice on the cross.

True love in marriage requires more than affection—it demands sacrifice, humility, and a commitment to serve one another daily. Sacrificial love means laying down your desires, pride, and convenience for the good of your spouse, trusting that God's design for marriage is rooted in mutual love, respect, and selflessness. In the same way that Christ laid down His life for the church, we are called to lay down our lives for our spouse, creating a relationship that honors God and reflects His love for the world.

This week, we will explore what it means to truly love and sacrifice for your spouse in the context of marriage. Whether you're in a season of joy or challenge, sacrificial love will strengthen your marriage and draw you closer to God's design for this sacred union. Ask yourself: How can I love my spouse more selflessly, and in what ways can I sacrifice for the sake of our marriage? Remember, as you pour into your marriage with love and sacrifice, God will bless and sustain your relationship, helping you grow together in faith and unity.

- Focus: Understanding the husband's role to love sacrificially.
- Key Scripture: Ephesians 5:25-28

> *"25 Husbands, love your wives, just as Christ also loved the church and gave Himself up for her, 26 so that He might sanctify her, having cleansed her by the washing of water with the word, 27 that He might present to Himself the church in all her glory, having no spot or wrinkle or any such thing; but that she would be holy and blameless. 28 So husbands ought also to love their own wives as their own bodies. He who loves his own wife loves himself;"*

- Discussion Questions:

1. What does it mean to love your wife as Christ loved the church?

______________________________

______________________________

______________________________

______________________________

______________________________

______________________________

______________________________

2. How can you practically demonstrate sacrificial love to your spouse?

______________________________

______________________________

______________________________

______________________________

______________________________

______________________________

______________________________

- Action Step: Write down one specific way you can love and serve your wife this week in a Christlike manner.

- Man Up Challenge: Pray with your spouse daily this week, asking God to help you love her with sacrificial love. (Pray for Your Marriage and Relationship, Pray for Wisdom and Guidance, Pray for Each Other's Spiritual Growth, Pray for Protection Over Your Family, Pray for God's Purpose and Mission in Your Lives)

**Week 13 Bible Reading:** *Deuteronomy 16–34; Mark 9–10*

**Week 13 Accountability Questions for You and/ or Your Group: (End each week, holding each other accountable with these questions. Be honest, this is where we grow.)**

| | | Yes | No |
|---|---|---|---|
| 1. | Have you spent daily time in the Scriptures and in prayer? | | |
| 2. | Have you had any impure thoughts that would not glorify God? | | |
| 3. | Have you been completely above reproach in your financial dealings? | | |
| 4. | Have you spent quality relationship time with family and friends? | | |
| 5. | Have you done your 100% best in your job, school, home, etc.? | | |
| 6. | Have you told any half-truths or outright lies, putting yourself in a better light to those around you? | | |
| 7. | Have you shared the Gospel with an unbeliever this week? | | |
| 8. | Have you taken care of your body through daily physical exercise and proper eating/sleeping habits? | | |
| 9. | Have you allowed any person or circumstance to rob you of your joy? | | |
| 10. | Have you lied on any of your answers today? | | |

| **Prayer Request** | **Name 5 People To Pray for this Week** |
|---|---|
| • ______________________ | • ______________________ |
| • ______________________ | • ______________________ |
| • ______________________ | • ______________________ |
| • ______________________ | • ______________________ |
| • ______________________ | • ______________________ |
| • ______________________ | • ______________________ |
| • ______________________ | • ______________________ |

**Each week, we will give you men in the Bible who exemplified the main theme. Take time this week to study these men.**

**1. Boaz – Redeeming Love and Protection**

- Scripture: Ruth 4:9-10
  "Then Boaz said to the elders and all the people, 'You are witnesses today that I have bought from the hand of Naomi all that belonged to Elimelech and all that belonged to Chilion and Mahlon. Moreover, I have acquired Ruth the Moabitess, the widow of Mahlon, to be my wife in order to raise up the name of the deceased on his inheritance, so that the name of the deceased will not be cut off from his brothers or from the court of his birth place; you are witnesses today.'"

- Overview: Boaz exemplified sacrificial love by redeeming Ruth, a widow, and marrying her to provide for her and her family. His actions demonstrated not only love for Ruth but also an understanding of his responsibility to protect and provide for her in a time of vulnerability. Boaz's willingness to step in and take on this responsibility shows selflessness and godly love.

**2. Jacob – Persevering in Love through Sacrifice**

- Scripture: Genesis 29:20
  "So Jacob served seven years for Rachel and they seemed to him but a few days because of his love for her."

- Overview: Jacob's love for Rachel led him to sacrifice years of his life in service to her father, Laban, to earn her hand in marriage. Even when Laban deceived him by giving Leah as a wife first, Jacob continued to serve another seven years for Rachel. His perseverance and commitment to Rachel exemplify a love that is willing to sacrifice time, effort, and personal comfort for the one he loved.

3. Elkanah – Loving Sacrifice and Support for Hannah

- Scripture: 1 Samuel 1:8
  "Then Elkanah her husband said to her, 'Hannah, why do you weep and why do you not eat and why is your heart sad? Am I not better to you than ten sons?'"

- Overview: Elkanah's love for his wife, Hannah, is evident in how he supported and comforted her through her deep distress over her inability to have children. Though he could have been content with his other wife and children, Elkanah showed love and sacrifice by caring for Hannah's emotional and spiritual needs, going with her to the temple and offering support during a painful season in their marriage.

*"True love in marriage is not about what you can get, but about what you're willing to give. Sacrifice is the foundation of a godly marriage—putting your spouse's needs above your own and choosing to love selflessly, just as Christ loved us."- Jody Burkeen*

# UNDERSTANDING AND HONORING YOUR WIFE

## WEEK 14: UNDERSTANDING AND HONORING YOUR WIFE

The Bible calls husbands not only to love their wives but to live with them in an understanding way, showing them honor and respect. In 1 Peter 3:7, it says, *"You husbands in the same way, live with your wives in an understanding way, as with someone weaker, since she is a woman; and show her honor as a fellow heir of the grace of life, so that your prayers will not be hindered."* This verse reveals the importance of both understanding and honoring your wife as a crucial part of a godly marriage.

Understanding your wife goes beyond knowing her likes and dislikes—it means taking the time to listen, empathize, and seek to meet her needs on a deeper level. Honoring her means valuing her as an equal partner in God's kingdom and treating her with the love, respect, and care she deserves. When you make the effort to understand and honor your wife, you reflect God's love for her and build a stronger, more resilient marriage.

This week, we'll explore what it truly means to understand and honor your wife, looking at practical ways to apply these biblical principles in your relationship. Ask yourself: Am I actively listening to my wife's needs, fears, and dreams? How can I show her that I value and honor her as God does? As you grow in your ability to understand and honor your wife, you'll find that your marriage becomes a greater source of joy, unity, and spiritual strength.

- Focus: Leading with understanding and honor in marriage.
- Key Scripture: 1 Peter 3:7

> *" You husbands in the same way, live with your wives in an understanding way, as with someone weaker, since she is a woman; and show her honor as a fellow heir of the grace of life, so that your prayers will not be hindered."*

- Discussion Questions:

1. What does it mean to live with your wife in an understanding way?

2. How can showing honor to your wife improve your leadership in the home?

3. If you don't know how to honor your wife, ask her what ways you could honor her.

- Action Step: Take time this week to have an open conversation with your wife about her needs and how you can better understand and support her.

- Man Up Challenge: Make a commitment to honor your wife in a specific way this week, whether it's through words of affirmation, acts of service, or another meaningful action.

**Week 14 Bible Reading**: *Joshua 1–15; Mark 11–12*

**Week 14 Accountability Questions for You and/ or Your Group: (End each week, holding each other accountable with these questions. Be honest, this is where we grow.)**

| | | Yes | No |
|---|---|---|---|
| 1. | Have you spent daily time in the Scriptures and in prayer? | | |
| 2. | Have you had any impure thoughts that would not glorify God? | | |
| 3. | Have you been completely above reproach in your financial dealings? | | |
| 4. | Have you spent quality relationship time with family and friends? | | |
| 5. | Have you done your 100% best in your job, school, home, etc.? | | |
| 6. | Have you told any half-truths or outright lies, putting yourself in a better light to those around you? | | |
| 7. | Have you shared the Gospel with an unbeliever this week? | | |
| 8. | Have you taken care of your body through daily physical exercise and proper eating/sleeping habits? | | |
| 9. | Have you allowed any person or circumstance to rob you of your joy? | | |
| 10. | Have you lied on any of your answers today? | | |

**Prayer Request**

- ____________________
- ____________________
- ____________________
- ____________________
- ____________________
- ____________________
- ____________________

**Name 5 People To Pray for this Week**

- ____________________
- ____________________
- ____________________
- ____________________
- ____________________
- ____________________
- ____________________

Each week, we will give you men in the Bible who exemplified the main theme. Take time this week to study these men.

**1. Elkanah – Supportive and Compassionate with Hannah**

- Scripture: 1 Samuel 1:8
  "Then Elkanah her husband said to her, 'Hannah, why do you weep and why do you not eat and why is your heart sad? Am I not better to you than ten sons?'"

- Overview: Elkanah demonstrated understanding and compassion toward his wife, Hannah, when she was deeply grieved over her inability to have children. He showed her kindness, support, and tried to reassure her of his love, even when she was consumed by sorrow. While he may not have fully understood her pain, he honored her by comforting her and being patient with her struggles.

**2. Boaz – Respectful and Honorable with Ruth**

- Scripture: Ruth 2:11-12
  "Boaz replied to her, 'All that you have done for your mother-in-law after the death of your husband has been fully reported to me, and how you left your father and your mother and the land of your birth, and came to a people that you did not previously know. May the Lord reward your work, and your wages be full from the Lord, the God of Israel, under whose wings you have come to seek refuge.'"

- Overview: Boaz showed respect and honor to Ruth by acknowledging her character, providing for her needs, and protecting her reputation. He went above and beyond to ensure her well-being, ultimately redeeming her and bringing her into his family. His actions exemplified a man who honored Ruth's worth and treated her with dignity and kindness.

**3. Joseph – Honoring Mary Despite Personal Cost**

- Scripture: Matthew 1:19
  "And Joseph her husband, being a righteous man and not wanting to disgrace her, planned to send her away secretly."

- Overview: When Joseph learned that Mary was pregnant before they were married, he could have exposed her to public shame. However, he chose to act in a way that would protect her dignity and honor. Even before he understood the full situation, Joseph showed compassion and respect toward Mary, demonstrating his commitment to honoring her. After receiving God's guidance, he fully embraced his role as her husband and the earthly father of Jesus.

> *"Loving your wife means honoring her with your words, actions, and the way you prioritize her. To understand her is to serve her with empathy, treating her with the same grace God shows us."— James Dobson*

# LEADING AND DISCIPLING YOUR CHILDREN

## WEEK 15: LEADING AND DISCIPLING YOUR CHILDREN

As a father, one of your greatest responsibilities is to lead and disciple your children in the ways of the Lord. The Bible calls parents to teach, guide, and model a life of faith for their children, helping them grow into a relationship with God that will last a lifetime. Proverbs 22:6 reminds us, *"Train up a child in the way he should go, even when he is old he will not depart from it."* This calling isn't just about teaching morals but about instilling a faith that is real, personal, and transformative.

Discipling your children means actively and intentionally pointing them to Christ through both words and actions. It involves praying with them, teaching them Scripture, and modeling godly character in your daily life. When you lead by example, you give your children a blueprint for a faith that endures. This kind of leadership requires patience, consistency, and a willingness to learn alongside them as you grow in your walk with God.

This week, we will explore what it means to lead and disciple your children, looking at biblical principles and practical ways to nurture their spiritual growth. Ask yourself: Am I investing in my children's spiritual lives as much as in their physical and emotional well-being? How can I create opportunities for them to encounter God personally? As you embrace this role, remember that God equips you to be the spiritual leader your children need, guiding them toward a faith that will sustain them throughout their lives.

- Focus: The father's role in spiritually leading his children.
- Key Scripture: Proverbs 22:6

> *" Train up a child in the way he should go, even when he is old he will not depart from it."*

- Discussion Questions:

1. How can you disciple your children and raise them according to God's principles?

2. What spiritual habits can you cultivate in your children to help them grow in their faith?

- Action Step: Set a spiritual goal for your family, such as starting family devotions, praying together, or teaching your children a biblical truth each week.

- Man Up Challenge: Pray with your children daily this week. Encourage them to share their own prayers and discuss how God answers prayer in your family life.

**Week 15 Bible Reading**: *Joshua 16–24; Judges 1–8; Mark 13–14*

**Week 15 Accountability Questions for You and/ or Your Group: (End each week, holding each other accountable with these questions. Be honest, this is where we grow.)**

| | | Yes | No |
|---|---|---|---|
| 1. | Have you spent daily time in the Scriptures and in prayer? | | |
| 2. | Have you had any impure thoughts that would not glorify God? | | |
| 3. | Have you been completely above reproach in your financial dealings? | | |
| 4. | Have you spent quality relationship time with family and friends? | | |
| 5. | Have you done your 100% best in your job, school, home, etc.? | | |
| 6. | Have you told any half-truths or outright lies, putting yourself in a better light to those around you? | | |
| 7. | Have you shared the Gospel with an unbeliever this week? | | |
| 8. | Have you taken care of your body through daily physical exercise and proper eating/sleeping habits? | | |
| 9. | Have you allowed any person or circumstance to rob you of your joy? | | |
| 10. | Have you lied on any of your answers today? | | |

**Prayer Request**

- ______________________________
- ______________________________
- ______________________________
- ______________________________
- ______________________________
- ______________________________
- ______________________________

**Name 5 People To Pray for this Week**

- ______________________________
- ______________________________
- ______________________________
- ______________________________
- ______________________________
- ______________________________
- ______________________________

**Each week, we will give you men in the Bible who exemplified the main theme. Take time this week to study these men.**

### 1. Abraham – A Father of Faith Who Led His Household

- Scripture: Genesis 18:19
  "For I have chosen him, so that he may command his children and his household after him to keep the way of the Lord by doing righteousness and justice, so that the Lord may bring upon Abraham what He has spoken about him."

- Overview: Abraham demonstrated faith in God and a commitment to leading his family in righteousness. God chose Abraham because he would instruct his children and household to follow the Lord. Abraham's example of obedience, trust, and faith became a legacy for future generations, ultimately blessing his descendants.

### 2. Noah – A Righteous Man Who Guided His Family through Obedience

- Scripture: Genesis 7:1
  "Then the Lord said to Noah, 'Enter the ark, you and all your household, for you alone I have seen to be righteous before Me in this time.'"

- Overview: Noah showed leadership by obeying God's commands, even when it went against the norms of his culture. He led his family in faith by building the ark, trusting God's word, and guiding them to safety. His obedience and faithfulness were crucial in saving his family and preserving their relationship with God.

### 3. Joshua – A Leader Who Declared His Family's Commitment to God

- Scripture: Joshua 24:15
  "If it is disagreeable in your sight to serve the Lord, choose for yourselves today whom you will serve... but as for me and my house, we will serve the Lord."

- Overview: Joshua exemplified strong spiritual leadership by declaring his household's commitment to serve God. He wasn't content to let his family follow any path; he intentionally led them in a covenant relationship with God. Joshua's firm declaration showed his resolve to disciple his family and hold them accountable to a life dedicated to God.

*Callout "Your role as a father isn't just to raise good kids; it's to raise godly kids. Leading and discipling your children means showing them what it looks like to follow Christ daily, teaching them that faith isn't just talked about but lived out."— Jody Burkeen*

# SETTING A GODLY EXAMPLE IN THE HOME

## WEEK 16: SETTING A GODLY EXAMPLE IN THE HOME

As a husband and father, you are called to be a living example of faith, integrity, and godliness for your family. In the home, your actions, attitudes, and words create the foundation for how your family understands and experiences God's love and truth. Proverbs 20:7 says, *"A righteous man who walks in his integrity—how blessed are his sons after him."* Setting a godly example isn't just about what you teach; it's about how you live, modeling a faith that is authentic, steadfast, and grounded in God's Word.

Being a godly example means practicing humility, patience, love, and self-control in your daily life. It's leading by serving, forgiving, and putting others before yourself. When your family sees you actively seeking God, praying, and living out your faith with consistency, it inspires them to follow that same path. This type of leadership requires intentionality, as it calls you to live out your faith even in the small, everyday moments—when you're tired, challenged, or in the face of difficulty.

This week, we'll explore what it means to set a godly example in your home, looking at practical ways to reflect Christ's character in every interaction. Ask yourself: Am I living in a way that points my family to God? How can I better model the love, strength, and wisdom that God desires? By embracing this call, you'll leave a lasting legacy of faith that shapes and strengthens your family for generations.

- **Focus:** Living as a godly example for your family to follow.
- **Key Scriptures:** Ephesians 5:25-28, 1 Peter 3:7
- **Discussion Questions:**

1. How can you model godliness, integrity, and faithfulness for your wife and children?

2. What areas of your personal life need to be strengthened so you can lead your family well?

- **Action Step:** Write out a personal spiritual goal that will help you grow as a leader in your home. Share this goal with your family for accountability.

- **Man Up Challenge:** Take action this week to lead by example in one specific area, such as prayer, Bible study, integrity, or service. Demonstrate to your family how to follow Christ through your actions.

**Week 16 Bible Reading**: *Judges 9–21; Mark 15–16*

## Using the 22 Questions for Accountability

John Wesley and his Holy Club were renowned for their dedication to spiritual growth and rigorous accountability. At the heart of their gatherings were 22 questions that challenged each member to examine their faith, actions, and intentions. These questions were designed to help men remain focused on their walk with Christ, to grow in holiness, and to hold each other accountable to living out the Gospel daily.

In a world full of distractions and temptations, it's easy to drift in our spiritual lives without even realizing it. The 22 questions serve as a powerful tool to bring us back into alignment with God's will and to cultivate a life of intentional faith. They cover areas such as integrity, personal holiness, and commitment to spiritual disciplines, calling us to examine our hearts deeply and honestly.

Using these questions for accountability, whether in a group setting or personal reflection, can strengthen your walk with Christ by fostering humility, transparency, and a commitment to spiritual growth. As we go through these questions, consider how they apply to your life and how you can use them to grow as a man of God. True accountability isn't just about pointing out faults; it's about walking alongside one another, encouraging one another, and pushing one another toward holiness.

In your final week for this session, we encourage you to reflect on these questions with a trusted brother in Christ. Reflect and review the past four weeks and check your **prayer request** and the people you are praying for. Did you see God move? Allow these questions to challenge you to greater faithfulness, as they have for countless men of faith through the centuries.

1. Am I consciously or unconsciously creating the impression that I am better than I really am? In other words, am I a hypocrite?
2. Am I honest in all my acts and words, or do I exaggerate?
3. Do I confidentially pass on to another what was told to me in confidence?
4. Can I be trusted?
5. Am I a slave to dress, friends, work, or habits?
6. Am I self-conscious, self-pitying, or self-justifying?
7. Did the Bible live in me today?

8. Do I give it time to speak to me everyday?
9. Am I enjoying prayer?
10. When did I last speak to someone else about my faith?
11. Do I pray about the money I spend?
12. Do I get to bed on time and get up on time?
13. Do I disobey God in anything?
14. Do I insist upon doing something about which my conscience is uneasy?
15. Am I defeated in any part of my life?
16. Am I jealous, impure, critical, irritable, touchy, or distrustful?
17. How do I spend my spare time?
18. Am I proud?
19. Do I thank God that I am not as other people, especially as the Pharisees who despised the publican?
20. Is there anyone whom I fear, dislike, disown, criticize, hold a resentment toward or disregard? If so, what am I doing about it?
21. Do I grumble or complain constantly?
22. Is Christ real to me?

# CHAPTER 5

# OVERCOMING TEMPTATION

# UNDERSTANDING TEMPTATION

## WEEK 17: UNDERSTANDING TEMPTATION

Temptation is a reality that every believer faces, yet it's essential to understand that temptation itself is not sin; rather, it's the crossroads where we choose either to follow God's way or yield to the desires of the flesh. The Bible tells us in 1 Corinthians 10:13 , *"No temptation has overtaken you but such as is common to man; and God is faithful, who will not allow you to be tempted beyond what you are able, but with the temptation will provide the way of escape also so that you will be able to endure it."* God assures us that while temptation is inevitable, He always provides us with the strength and means to resist.

Understanding temptation means recognizing its sources, whether it's from the enemy, the world around us, or our own desires. It also means being aware of our vulnerabilities and staying alert to situations that can lead us astray. Temptation often disguises itself as something desirable or seemingly harmless, so discerning its true nature requires wisdom, prayer, and a commitment to God's Word. By understanding how temptation works, we can prepare to face it with courage and rely on God's power to overcome it.

This week, we will explore the nature of temptation, why we face it, and how we can stand firm against it. Reflect on where you may be most susceptible and ask yourself: Am I relying on my own strength, or am I leaning into God's help and guidance? As we grow in understanding, we can walk in greater victory, trusting that God will provide the way to resist and remain faithful.

- Focus: Recognizing the nature of temptation and where it comes from.
- Key Scripture: James 1:12-15

> *"Blessed is a man who perseveres under trial; for once he has been approved, he will receive the crown of life which the Lord has promised to those who love Him. Let no one say when he is tempted, "I am being tempted by God"; for God cannot be tempted by evil, and He Himself does not tempt anyone. But each one is tempted when he is carried away and enticed by his own lust. Then when lust has conceived, it gives birth to sin; and when sin is accomplished, it brings forth death. Do not be deceived, my beloved brethren."*

- Discussion Questions:

1. How does James describe the process of temptation turning into sin?

2. What desires in your life could lead to temptation?

- Action Step: Take time to reflect on areas of your life where you are most vulnerable to temptation. Identify the desires that could lead to sinful actions.

- Man Up Challenge: Memorize James 1:12-15 this week. Ask God to help you recognize the early stages of temptation and respond with wisdom.

**Week 17 Bible Reading:** *Ruth 1–4; 1 Samuel 1–15; Luke 1–2*

**Week 17- Accountability Questions for You and/ or Your Group: (End each week, holding each other accountable with these questions. Be honest, this is where we grow.)**

| | | Yes | No |
|---|---|---|---|
| 1. | Have you spent daily time in the Scriptures and in prayer? | | |
| 2. | Have you had any impure thoughts that would not glorify God? | | |
| 3. | Have you been completely above reproach in your financial dealings? | | |
| 4. | Have you spent quality relationship time with family and friends? | | |
| 5. | Have you done your 100% best in your job, school, home, etc.? | | |
| 6. | Have you told any half-truths or outright lies, putting yourself in a better light to those around you? | | |
| 7. | Have you shared the Gospel with an unbeliever this week? | | |
| 8. | Have you taken care of your body through daily physical exercise and proper eating/sleeping habits? | | |
| 9. | Have you allowed any person or circumstance to rob you of your joy? | | |
| 10. | Have you lied on any of your answers today? | | |

| **Prayer Request** | **Name 5 People To Pray for this Week** |
|---|---|
| • ________________ | • ________________ |
| • ________________ | • ________________ |
| • ________________ | • ________________ |
| • ________________ | • ________________ |
| • ________________ | • ________________ |
| • ________________ | • ________________ |
| • ________________ | • ________________ |

Each week, we will give you men in the Bible who exemplified the main theme. Take time this week to study these men.

1. **Joseph – Resisting Temptation through Integrity and Fear of God**

    - **Scripture:** Genesis 39:7-10
    *"It came about after these events that his master's wife looked with desire at Joseph, and she said, 'Lie with me.' But he refused and said to his master's wife, 'Behold, with me here, my master does not concern himself with anything in the house... How then could I do this great evil and sin against God?'"*

    - **Overview:** Joseph exemplified an understanding of temptation by recognizing it and responding with integrity. When tempted by Potiphar's wife, Joseph understood the consequences and sin involved and immediately rejected her advances, choosing to honor God rather than yield to temptation. His fear of God and commitment to righteousness helped him resist a potentially destructive path.

2. **Jesus – Confronting Temptation with God's Word**

    - **Scripture:** Matthew 4:1-11
    *"Then Jesus was led up by the Spirit into the wilderness to be tempted by the devil. And after He had fasted forty days and forty nights, He then became hungry. And the tempter came and said to Him, 'If You are the Son of God, command that these stones become bread.'"*

    - **Overview:** Jesus faced direct temptation from Satan in the wilderness, yet each time, He responded with Scripture. His example shows that understanding temptation involves knowing God's truth and using it as a defense against deception. Jesus' resistance to the enemy's tactics shows us the power of relying on God's Word to withstand temptation.

3. **David – Learning from Failure in the Face of Temptation**

    - **Scripture:** 2 Samuel 11:2-4
    *"Now when evening came David arose from his bed and walked around on the roof of the king's house, and from the roof he saw a woman bathing; and the woman was very beautiful in appearance. So David sent and inquired about the woman. And one said, 'Is this not Bathsheba, the daughter of Eliam, the wife of Uriah the Hittite?'"*

- **Overview:** David's encounter with temptation and subsequent fall in the matter of Bathsheba is a sobering example of what can happen when we give in to temptation. Though David initially failed, he later repented deeply (Psalm 51). His story demonstrates that understanding temptation includes acknowledging our own weaknesses and seeking God's forgiveness and restoration when we stumble.

> **Callout** *"Temptation isn't a sign that you're weak; it's a reminder that you're human. The strength to overcome it doesn't come from within us but from the power of Christ working in us."*— ***Charles Stanley***

# GOD'S FAITHFULNESS IN TEMPTATION

## WEEK 18: GOD'S FAITHFULNESS IN TEMPTATION

When we face temptation, it can feel overwhelming, as though we are alone in our struggle. Yet, the Bible assures us that God is not distant or indifferent to our challenges; He is faithful and present, offering strength and a way out. 1 Corinthians 10:13 (NASB) reminds us, *"No temptation has overtaken you but such as is common to man; and God is faithful, who will not allow you to be tempted beyond what you are able, but with the temptation will provide the way of escape also, so that you will be able to endure it."* God promises that He will not allow us to face more than we can bear and that He will provide a path to resist and overcome.

God's faithfulness in temptation is rooted in His understanding of our weaknesses and His deep love for us. He doesn't leave us to fight alone; instead, He empowers us through His Word, the guidance of the Holy Spirit, and the strength found in prayer. Knowing that God is faithful allows us to face temptation with confidence, not in our own strength but in His. He is always ready to help us stand firm, no matter how strong the pull of temptation may feel.

This week, we will explore God's role in helping us withstand temptation, focusing on His promises, provision, and protection. As you reflect, consider how you can lean on God's faithfulness when temptation arises. Ask yourself: Am I trusting God to guide me through temptation, or am I relying solely on my own willpower? Remember, God's faithfulness means that you are never alone in your struggles, and He will always provide the strength to overcome.

- Focus: Trusting God's promise to provide a way out of temptation.
- Key Scripture: 1 Corinthians 10:13

> *" No temptation has overtaken you but such as is common to man; and God is faithful, who will not allow you to be tempted beyond what you are able, but with the temptation will provide the way of escape also, so that you will be able to endure it..."*

- Discussion Questions:

1. What does it mean that God will not allow you to be tempted beyond what you can bear?

2. How can you recognize the "way out" that God provides during temptation?

3. Name some ways to stop temptation when you are faced with it? Lust? Anger? Pride? Worry?

- Action Step: Reflect on moments when you've faced temptation and failed to look for God's "way out." This week, be intentional about watching for the escape routes God provides.

- Man Up Challenge: Each day, pray for wisdom to recognize the way out when facing temptation. Keep 1 Corinthians 10:13 in mind during moments of temptation.

**Week 18 `Bible Reading:** *1 Samuel 16–31; 2 Samuel 1–10; Luke 3–4*

**Week 18- Accountability Questions for You and/ or Your Group: (End each week, holding each other accountable with these questions. Be honest, this is where we grow.)**

| | | Yes | No |
|---|---|---|---|
| 1. | Have you spent daily time in the Scriptures and in prayer? | | |
| 2. | Have you had any impure thoughts that would not glorify God? | | |
| 3. | Have you been completely above reproach in your financial dealings? | | |
| 4. | Have you spent quality relationship time with family and friends? | | |
| 5. | Have you done your 100% best in your job, school, home, etc.? | | |
| 6. | Have you told any half-truths or outright lies, putting yourself in a better light to those around you? | | |
| 7. | Have you shared the Gospel with an unbeliever this week? | | |
| 8. | Have you taken care of your body through daily physical exercise and proper eating/sleeping habits? | | |
| 9. | Have you allowed any person or circumstance to rob you of your joy? | | |
| 10. | Have you lied on any of your answers today? | | |

**Prayer Request**

- ______________________
- ______________________
- ______________________
- ______________________
- ______________________
- ______________________
- ______________________

**Name 5 People To Pray for this Week**

- ______________________
- ______________________
- ______________________
- ______________________
- ______________________
- ______________________
- ______________________

**Each week, we will give you men in the Bible who exemplified the main theme. Take time this week to study these men.**

**1. Joseph – God's Presence and Provision Amidst Temptation**

- **Scripture:** Genesis 39:2-3
  *"The Lord was with Joseph, so he became a successful man. And he was in the house of his master, the Egyptian. Now his master saw that the Lord was with him and how the Lord caused all that he did to prosper in his hand."*

- **Overview:** Joseph faced intense temptation from Potiphar's wife, but he resisted because he recognized it would be a sin against God. God's faithfulness was evident in Joseph's life, even when he faced false accusations and imprisonment. Despite the challenges, God remained with Joseph, blessing him and eventually raising him to a position of authority in Egypt.

**2. Daniel – God's Protection Through Faithfulness in Temptation**

- **Scripture:** Daniel 6:22 raising him to an authority position
  *"My God sent His angel and shut the lions' mouths and they have not harmed me, inasmuch as I was found innocent before Him; and also toward you, O king, I have committed no crime."*

- **Overview:** Daniel was tempted to compromise his faith to avoid persecution. Instead, he remained steadfast in his commitment to praying to God, even when it meant being thrown into the lions' den. God's faithfulness was shown in protecting Daniel and delivering him unharmed, proving that He is with those who trust Him in the face of temptation.

3. **Jesus – God's Strength and Guidance in the Wilderness**

- **Scripture:** Matthew 4:10-11
  *"Then Jesus said to him, 'Go, Satan! For it is written, "You shall worship the Lord your God, and serve Him only."' Then the devil left Him; and behold, angels came and began to minister to Him."*

- **Overview:** Jesus faced direct temptation from Satan in the wilderness, but He relied on Scripture and God's guidance to resist. Each time Satan tempted Him, Jesus responded with God's Word, demonstrating God's faithfulness in providing the strength needed to overcome. After resisting temptation, Jesus was ministered to by angels, showing God's care and provision.

**Callout:** *"God's faithfulness doesn't mean you won't face temptation; it means you'll never face it alone. He stands with you, providing strength, guidance, and a way out, so you can walk in victory."* — ***Jody Burkeen***

# RESISTING TEMPTATION THROUGH SCRIPTURE

## WEEK 19: RESISTING TEMPTATION THROUGH SCRIPTURE

In the face of temptation, our greatest defense is God's Word. Scripture is more than just words on a page; it's a powerful weapon that equips us to stand firm against the enemy's schemes. Jesus Himself demonstrated this truth during His time in the wilderness. When Satan tempted Him, Jesus responded each time with Scripture, saying, *"It is written..."* (Matthew 4:4, 7, 10). By relying on the truth of God's Word, Jesus set an example for us on how to resist temptation with strength and clarity.

Temptation often comes in moments of vulnerability, offering quick satisfaction or temporary relief. But Scripture reminds us of God's promises, His commands, and His purpose for our lives. By filling our hearts and minds with His Word, we're better prepared to recognize the lies of temptation and counter them with truth. Memorizing and meditating on Scripture strengthens our spiritual foundation, allowing us to respond decisively when temptation arises.

This week, we will explore how Scripture helps us resist temptation and how to incorporate it into our daily lives as a spiritual defense. Consider: Are you equipping yourself with God's Word to withstand temptation? How can you make Scripture a more active part of your life to guard against the enemy's attacks? As we delve into the power of Scripture, remember that God's Word is your shield, providing guidance and strength to live victoriously.

- **Focus:** Using Scripture to stand strong against temptation.
- **Key Scripture:** Matthew 4:1-11

> *Jesus' temptation in the wilderness shows the power of Scripture in resisting temptation.*

- **Discussion Questions:**

1. How did Jesus use Scripture to resist the devil's temptations?

2. What role does memorizing and meditating on Scripture play in overcoming temptation?

3. Do you have a life verse? One that will help you in the moment of temptation. Take time to find your life verse and write it down.

- **Action Step:** Choose one or two verses that specifically address the area of temptation you struggle with most. Memorize these verses and recite them when tempted. Read Psalm 119:11and memorize it.

- **Man Up Challenge:** Write down the specific scriptures you've memorized and repeat them daily. Share them with your accountability partner for added support.

**Week 19 Bible reading**: *2 Samuel 11–24; Luke 5–6*

**Week 19- Accountability Questions for You and/ or Your Group: (End each week, holding each other accountable with these questions. Be honest, this is where we grow.)**

| | | Yes | No |
|---|---|---|---|
| 1. | Have you spent daily time in the Scriptures and in prayer? | | |
| 2. | Have you had any impure thoughts that would not glorify God? | | |
| 3. | Have you been completely above reproach in your financial dealings? | | |
| 4. | Have you spent quality relationship time with family and friends? | | |
| 5. | Have you done your 100% best in your job, school, home, etc.? | | |
| 6. | Have you told any half-truths or outright lies, putting yourself in a better light to those around you? | | |
| 7. | Have you shared the Gospel with an unbeliever this week? | | |
| 8. | Have you taken care of your body through daily physical exercise and proper eating/sleeping habits? | | |
| 9. | Have you allowed any person or circumstance to rob you of your joy? | | |
| 10. | Have you lied on any of your answers today? | | |

| **Prayer Request** | **Name 5 People To Pray for this Week** |
|---|---|
| • ______________________ | • ______________________ |
| • ______________________ | • ______________________ |
| • ______________________ | • ______________________ |
| • ______________________ | • ______________________ |
| • ______________________ | • ______________________ |
| • ______________________ | • ______________________ |
| • ______________________ | • ______________________ |

**Each week, we will give you men in the Bible who exemplified the main theme. Take time this week to study these men.**

**1. Joseph – God's Presence and Provision Amidst Temptation**

- **Scripture:** Genesis 39:2-3
*"The Lord was with Joseph, so he became a successful man. And he was in the house of his master, the Egyptian. Now his master saw that the Lord was with him and how the Lord caused all that he did to prosper in his hand."*

- **Overview:** Joseph faced intense temptation from Potiphar's wife, but he resisted because he recognized it would be a sin against God. God's faithfulness was evident in Joseph's life, even when he faced false accusations and imprisonment. Despite the challenges, God remained with Joseph, blessing him and eventually raising him to a position of authority in Egypt.

**2. Daniel – God's Protection Through Faithfulness in Temptation**

- **Scripture:** Daniel 6:22 raising him to an authority position
*"My God sent His angel and shut the lions' mouths and they have not harmed me, inasmuch as I was found innocent before Him; and also toward you, O king, I have committed no crime."*

- **Overview:** Daniel was tempted to compromise his faith to avoid persecution. Instead, he remained steadfast in his commitment to praying to God, even when it meant being thrown into the lions' den. God's faithfulness was shown in protecting Daniel and delivering him unharmed, proving that He is with those who trust Him in the face of temptation.

**3. Jesus – God's Strength and Guidance in the Wilderness**

- **Scripture:** Matthew 4:10-11
*"Then Jesus said to him, 'Go, Satan! For it is written, "You shall worship the Lord your God, and serve Him only."' Then the devil left Him; and behold, angels came and began to minister to Him."*

- **Overview:** Jesus faced direct temptation from Satan in the wilderness, but He relied on Scripture and God's guidance to resist. Each time Satan tempted Him, Jesus responded with God's Word, demonstrating God's faithfulness in providing the strength needed to overcome. After resisting temptation, Jesus was ministered to by angels, showing God's care and provision.

> **Callout:** *"The Word of God is our greatest weapon against temptation. When we fill our minds with Scripture, we're equipping ourselves with truth that can cut through every lie the enemy throws our way."*— ***John MacArthur***

# DEVELOPING A PLAN FOR OVERCOMING TEMPTATION

## WEEK 20: DEVELOPING A PLAN FOR OVERCOMING TEMPTATION

Temptation is an inevitable part of life, but God calls us to prepare ourselves to stand firm when it arises. Overcoming temptation doesn't happen by accident—it requires intentionality, self-awareness, and reliance on God's guidance. Proverbs 4:26 says, *"Watch the path of your feet and all your ways will be established."* Developing a plan for overcoming temptation means being proactive in guarding your heart, mind, and actions, setting yourself up to make choices that honor God.

A plan for overcoming temptation involves several key components: recognizing your personal areas of weakness, setting boundaries, immersing yourself in God's Word, and staying accountable to trusted believers. By understanding where you're most vulnerable, you can take practical steps to avoid situations that may lead you astray. Additionally, turning to Scripture and prayer strengthens your resolve, reminding you of God's promises and His power to help you resist.

This week, we'll explore how to create a personal plan for overcoming temptation, focusing on practical tools and spiritual disciplines to help you stand strong. Reflect on where you struggle most and ask yourself: What boundaries do I need in place? How can I make God's Word and prayer a consistent part of my defense? Remember, with God's help and a thoughtful plan, you can face temptation with confidence and walk in victory.

- **Focus:** Creating a practical plan to resist temptation and pursue holiness.
- **Key Scriptures:** 1 Corinthians 10:13, James 1:12-15
- **Discussion Questions:**

1. What practical steps can you take to avoid situations that lead to temptation?

2. How can accountability with others help you stay strong in moments of weakness?

3. Talk with your group about areas in which you need accountability.

- **Action Step:** Develop a personal plan to resist temptation, which includes avoiding triggering situations, relying on Scripture, and having an accountability partner. " I have my answer ready before I am confronted with temptation, If I travel, I don't eat in hotel restaurants or bars, I don't ride in an elevator with a woman or allow myself alone with a woman. I don't text or call a woman without my wife in the room or on the text" – Jody Burkeen

- **Man Up Challenge:** Share your plan with a trusted friend or accountability partner. Commit to meeting regularly to check in on each other's progress in overcoming temptation.

**Week 20 bible reading***: 1 Kings 1–14; Luke 7–8*

## Using the 22 Questions for Accountability

John Wesley and his Holy Club were renowned for their dedication to spiritual growth and rigorous accountability. At the heart of their gatherings were 22 questions that challenged each member to examine their faith, actions, and intentions. These questions were designed to help men remain focused on their walk with Christ, to grow in holiness, and to hold each other accountable to living out the Gospel daily.

In a world full of distractions and temptations, it's easy to drift in our spiritual lives without even realizing it. The 22 questions serve as a powerful tool to bring us back into alignment with God's will and to cultivate a life of intentional faith. They cover areas such as integrity, personal holiness, and commitment to spiritual disciplines, calling us to examine our hearts deeply and honestly.

Using these questions for accountability, whether in a group setting or personal reflection, can strengthen your walk with Christ by fostering humility, transparency, and a commitment to spiritual growth. As we go through these questions, consider how they apply to your life and how you can use them to grow as a man of God. True accountability isn't just about pointing out faults; it's about walking alongside one another, encouraging one another, and pushing one another toward holiness.

In your final week for this session, we encourage you to reflect on these questions with a trusted brother in Christ. Reflect and review the past four weeks and check your **prayer request** and the people you are praying for. Did you see God move? Allow these questions to challenge you to greater faithfulness, as they have for countless men of faith through the centuries.

1. Am I consciously or unconsciously creating the impression that I am better than I really am? In other words, am I a hypocrite?
2. Am I honest in all my acts and words, or do I exaggerate?
3. Do I confidentially pass on to another what was told to me in confidence?
4. Can I be trusted?
5. Am I a slave to dress, friends, work, or habits?
6. Am I self-conscious, self-pitying, or self-justifying?
7. Did the Bible live in me today?

8. Do I give it time to speak to me everyday?
9. Am I enjoying prayer?
10. When did I last speak to someone else about my faith?
11. Do I pray about the money I spend?
12. Do I get to bed on time and get up on time?
13. Do I disobey God in anything?
14. Do I insist upon doing something about which my conscience is uneasy?
15. Am I defeated in any part of my life?
16. Am I jealous, impure, critical, irritable, touchy, or distrustful?
17. How do I spend my spare time?
18. Am I proud?
19. Do I thank God that I am not as other people, especially as the Pharisees who despised the publican?
20. Is there anyone whom I fear, dislike, disown, criticize, hold a resentment toward or disregard? If so, what am I doing about it?
21. Do I grumble or complain constantly?
22. Is Christ real to me?

*Callout- "Overcoming temptation requires more than just willpower; it demands a plan. When you equip yourself with God's Word, accountability, and a clear strategy, you're setting yourself up to walk in victory."*— **Jody Burkeen**

# CHAPTER 6
# PURSUING PURITY

# THE HEART OF PURITY

## WEEK 21: THE HEART OF PURITY

Purity goes beyond mere actions—it's a matter of the heart. True purity is about aligning our inner thoughts, desires, and motives with God's standards, allowing Him to transform us from the inside out. In Matthew 5:8 (NASB), Jesus says, "Blessed are the pure in heart, for they shall see God." This verse reveals that purity is not just about outward behavior; it's about cultivating a heart that seeks God above all else, leading to a life that honors Him in every area.

Living with a heart of purity means constantly examining our intentions, guarding our minds, and turning away from anything that would pull us away from God's presence. It requires daily surrender, choosing to let God shape our character and remove anything that hinders our relationship with Him. Pursuing purity is not easy in a world filled with distractions and temptations, but God calls us to set ourselves apart and reflect His holiness.

This week, we'll explore what it means to develop a heart of purity, focusing on both practical steps and spiritual disciplines that help us stay close to God. Ask yourself: Am I seeking purity in my thoughts, relationships, and actions? How can I invite God to refine my heart daily? As you pursue purity, remember that it's about drawing closer to God, allowing His presence to fill your life with purpose and peace.

- Focus: Understanding that purity begins in the heart.
- Key Scripture: Matthew 5:27-28

> *"27 "You have heard that it was said, 'You shall not commit adultery'; 28 but I say to you that everyone who looks at a woman with lust for her has already committed adultery with her in his heart.."*

- Discussion Questions:

1. Why does Jesus emphasize purity not just in actions but also in the heart?

_______________

_______________

_______________

_______________

_______________

2. How does lust affect our thoughts and actions, even if we don't act on it physically?

_______________

_______________

_______________

_______________

_______________

3. What material things get in the way of a pure heart? Phone? Computer? Gym? List some ways you can overcome the lust in these areas?

_______________

_______________

_______________

_______________

_______________

- Action Step: Reflect on the ways that lust or impure thoughts have affected your life. Commit to taking captive every thought and submitting it to Christ.

- Man Up Challenge: Memorize Matthew 5:27-28 and make a commitment to practice purity not only in your actions but in your thoughts. Start each day with a prayer for a pure heart.

**Week 21 Bible Reading**: *1 Kings 15–22; 2 Kings 1–10; Luke 9–10*

**Week 21- Accountability Questions for You and/ or Your Group: (End each week, holding each other accountable with these questions. Be honest, this is where we grow.)**

| | | Yes | No |
|---|---|---|---|
| 1. | Have you spent daily time in the Scriptures and in prayer? | | |
| 2. | Have you had any impure thoughts that would not glorify God? | | |
| 3. | Have you been completely above reproach in your financial dealings? | | |
| 4. | Have you spent quality relationship time with family and friends? | | |
| 5. | Have you done your 100% best in your job, school, home, etc.? | | |
| 6. | Have you told any half-truths or outright lies, putting yourself in a better light to those around you? | | |
| 7. | Have you shared the Gospel with an unbeliever this week? | | |
| 8. | Have you taken care of your body through daily physical exercise and proper eating/sleeping habits? | | |
| 9. | Have you allowed any person or circumstance to rob you of your joy? | | |
| 10. | Have you lied on any of your answers today? | | |

**Prayer Request**

- ____________________
- ____________________
- ____________________
- ____________________
- ____________________
- ____________________
- ____________________

**Name 5 People To Pray for this Week**

- ____________________
- ____________________
- ____________________
- ____________________
- ____________________
- ____________________
- ____________________

**Each week, we will give you men in the Bible who exemplified the main theme. Take time this week to study these men.**

**1. Joseph – A Commitment to Purity Despite Temptation**

- **Scripture:** Genesis 39:7-9
*"It came about after these events that his master's wife looked with desire at Joseph, and she said, 'Lie with me.' But he refused and said to his master's wife, 'Behold, with me here, my master does not concern himself with anything in the house, and he has put all that he owns in my charge... How then could I do this great evil and sin against God?'"*

- **Overview:** Joseph displayed a heart of purity by refusing to give in to the advances of Potiphar's wife. His commitment to purity was rooted in his desire to honor God above all else. Joseph's response to temptation highlights his integrity and his deep understanding that true purity is about remaining faithful to God, even in private moments.

**2. Job – Choosing Purity in Thought and Action**

- **Scripture:** Job 31:1
*"I have made a covenant with my eyes; how then could I gaze at a virgin?"*

- **Overview:** Job's commitment to purity was both inward and outward. By making a covenant with his eyes, he demonstrated a proactive approach to guarding his heart and mind from impure thoughts. Job's example shows that a heart of purity involves intentional boundaries and a willingness to resist even the smallest compromises.

**3. David – Pursuing Purity and Repentance**

- **Scripture:** Psalm 51:10
*"Create in me a clean heart, O God, and renew a steadfast spirit within me."*

- **Overview:** After his sin with Bathsheba, David's prayer in Psalm 51 demonstrates his desire for a heart of purity and his recognition of the need for God's cleansing. David's example shows that even when we fall, a heart of purity is marked by repentance and a longing to be restored to right standing with God. His plea for a clean heart reveals a deep yearning for holiness and a life pleasing to God.

**Callout:** *"Purity is not just about what you avoid but about what you pursue. A heart of purity seeks God above all else, desiring to honor Him in thought, word, and deed."*— ***John Piper***

# GOD'S WILL FOR PURITY

## WEEK 22: GOD'S WILL FOR PURITY

Purity is more than a personal choice; it's a command and a calling from God for every believer. The Bible makes it clear that God desires us to live in purity, setting ourselves apart from the world's standards and dedicating our lives to Him. In 1 Thessalonians 4:3, Paul writes, *"For this is the will of God, your sanctification; that is, that you abstain from sexual immorality."* God's will for our lives includes a commitment to purity in every aspect—our thoughts, words, actions, and relationships.

Living in purity means understanding that our bodies and minds are sacred, meant to honor God. It's a daily decision to walk in holiness and reject anything that might corrupt or pull us away from Him. This kind of purity isn't just about behavior modification; it's about a transformation of the heart. When we commit to purity, we are choosing to reflect God's character, pursue His righteousness, and live in a way that aligns with His desires for us.

This week, we will explore what it means to follow God's will for purity, looking at practical steps for maintaining a pure heart and life. Reflect on your current choices and attitudes, and ask yourself: Am I fully committed to God's standard of purity, or am I allowing worldly influences to shape my actions? As we seek His will, remember that God provides the strength and grace we need to live a life that honors Him.

- **Focus:** Understanding that God calls us to live in sexual purity.

- **Key Scripture:** 1 Thessalonians 4:3-5

> *"For this is the will of God, your sanctification; that is, that you abstain from sexual immorality; 4 that each of you know how to possess his own vessel in sanctification and honor, 5 not in lustful passion, like the Gentiles who do not know God;"*

- **Discussion Questions:**

1. What does it mean to control your body in a holy and honorable way?

2. How can you develop self-control in the area of sexual purity?

- **Action Step:** Identify specific areas where you struggle with purity (e.g., media consumption, internet use, personal boundaries) and create a plan to set up safeguards.

- **Man Up Challenge:** Establish accountability measures this week (e.g., accountability software, trusted accountability partners) to help you maintain sexual purity. Commit to living a life that honors God in body and mind.

**Week 22 Bible Reading**: *2 Kings 11–25; Luke 11–12*

**Week 22- Accountability Questions for You and/ or Your Group: (End each week, holding each other accountable with these questions. Be honest, this is where we grow.)**

| | | Yes | No |
|---|---|---|---|
| 1. | Have you spent daily time in the Scriptures and in prayer? | | |
| 2. | Have you had any impure thoughts that would not glorify God? | | |
| 3. | Have you been completely above reproach in your financial dealings? | | |
| 4. | Have you spent quality relationship time with family and friends? | | |
| 5. | Have you done your 100% best in your job, school, home, etc.? | | |
| 6. | Have you told any half-truths or outright lies, putting yourself in a better light to those around you? | | |
| 7. | Have you shared the Gospel with an unbeliever this week? | | |
| 8. | Have you taken care of your body through daily physical exercise and proper eating/sleeping habits? | | |
| 9. | Have you allowed any person or circumstance to rob you of your joy? | | |
| 10. | Have you lied on any of your answers today? | | |

**Prayer Request**

- ____________________
- ____________________
- ____________________
- ____________________
- ____________________
- ____________________
- ____________________

**Name 5 People To Pray for this Week**

- ____________________
- ____________________
- ____________________
- ____________________
- ____________________
- ____________________
- ____________________

**Each week, we will give you men in the Bible who exemplified the main theme. Take time this week to study these men.**

**1. Joseph – Resisting Temptation to Honor God**

- **Scripture:** Genesis 39:7-9 (NASB)
  *"It came about after these events that his master's wife looked with desire at Joseph, and she said, 'Lie with me.' But he refused and said to his master's wife, 'Behold, with me here, my master does not concern himself with anything in the house... How then could I do this great evil and sin against God?'"*

- **Overview:** Joseph's commitment to purity is seen in his refusal of Potiphar's wife's advances. Despite being far from home and facing significant temptation, Joseph held fast to God's will for purity, understanding that giving in would be a sin against God. His actions show a deep respect for God's standards and a desire to remain pure, even at great personal cost.

**2. Job – Purity of Mind and Heart**

- **Scripture:** Job 31:1 (NASB)
  *"I have made a covenant with my eyes; how then could I gaze at a virgin?"*

- **Overview:** Job's commitment to purity extended beyond his actions to his thoughts and intentions. By making a covenant with his eyes, Job displayed his desire to live a life of integrity and honor God not just in his deeds but in his inner thoughts as well. This intentional approach to purity reflects God's will for believers to guard their hearts and minds from sin.

**3. Daniel – Choosing Purity in a Corrupt Culture**

- **Scripture:** Daniel 1:8 (NASB)
  *"But Daniel made up his mind that he would not defile himself with the king's choice food or with the wine which he drank; so he sought permission from the commander of the officials that he might not defile himself."*

- **Overview:** Daniel's commitment to purity was evident in his decision not to partake in the food and wine from the king's table, which would have gone against his convictions and God's laws. Living in a foreign land where he could have easily adopted the surrounding culture's practices, Daniel chose instead to honor God by remaining pure in his actions and decisions.

> *"Purity isn't just about avoiding what's wrong; it's about pursuing what's right in God's eyes. Living in purity means aligning every part of your life—thoughts, actions, and intentions—with God's standards, not the world's."*— ***Jody Burkeen***

# FLEEING FROM SEXUAL IMMORALITY

## WEEK 23: FLEEING FROM SEXUAL IMMORALITY

In a world that often normalizes and even celebrates sexual immorality, God calls us to a different standard—to flee from it entirely. The Bible is clear in 1 Corinthians 6:18 (NASB): *"Flee immorality. Every other sin that a man commits is outside the body, but the immoral man sins against his own body."* This command to "flee" is not passive; it's an urgent call to actively avoid anything that can lead us into temptation or compromise our purity.

Fleeing from sexual immorality requires more than just willpower; it requires wisdom, boundaries, and a commitment to honoring God with our bodies and minds. This means not only avoiding overtly sinful actions but also guarding our hearts and minds from influences that can weaken our resolve. When we understand the impact of sexual sin—not only on ourselves but also on our relationship with God—it becomes clear why He calls us to pursue purity and to turn away from anything that can lead us astray.

This week, we'll explore practical steps for fleeing from sexual immorality, from setting boundaries to filling our minds with God's truth. Reflect on your own life and ask yourself: Am I creating an environment that honors God, or am I leaving room for temptation? Remember, God provides the strength and grace we need to flee sin and live lives that reflect His holiness.

- Focus: Learning to flee from situations that lead to impurity.
- Key Scripture: 1 Corinthians 6:18

> *"Flee immorality. Every other sin that a man commits is outside the body, but the immoral man sins against his own body.."*

- Discussion Questions:

1. Why does Paul command believers to flee from sexual immorality instead of resisting it?

2. What practical steps can you take to flee from situations that tempt you toward impurity?

- Action Step: Identify situations, environments, or habits that trigger impure thoughts or actions. Develop a strategy to avoid or flee from these temptations.

- Man Up Challenge: Create a plan to remove any stumbling blocks that lead to temptation (e.g., unfollowing certain social media accounts or avoiding specific environments). Commit to running toward purity by fleeing from temptation.

**Week 23 Bible Reading**: *1 Chronicles 1–15; Luke 13–14*

**Week 23- Accountability Questions for You and/ or Your Group: (End each week, holding each other accountable with these questions. Be honest, this is where we grow.)**

| | | Yes | No |
|---|---|---|---|
| 1. | Have you spent daily time in the Scriptures and in prayer? | | |
| 2. | Have you had any impure thoughts that would not glorify God? | | |
| 3. | Have you been completely above reproach in your financial dealings? | | |
| 4. | Have you spent quality relationship time with family and friends? | | |
| 5. | Have you done your 100% best in your job, school, home, etc.? | | |
| 6. | Have you told any half-truths or outright lies, putting yourself in a better light to those around you? | | |
| 7. | Have you shared the Gospel with an unbeliever this week? | | |
| 8. | Have you taken care of your body through daily physical exercise and proper eating/sleeping habits? | | |
| 9. | Have you allowed any person or circumstance to rob you of your joy? | | |
| 10. | Have you lied on any of your answers today? | | |

| **Prayer Request** | **Name 5 People To Pray for this Week** |
|---|---|
| • ______________________ | • ______________________ |
| • ______________________ | • ______________________ |
| • ______________________ | • ______________________ |
| • ______________________ | • ______________________ |
| • ______________________ | • ______________________ |
| • ______________________ | • ______________________ |
| • ______________________ | • ______________________ |

**Each week, we will give you men in the Bible who exemplified the main theme. Take time this week to study these men.**

### 1. JOSEPH – ACTIVELY FLEEING FROM TEMPTATION

- Scripture: Genesis 39:12
  "She caught him by his garment, saying, "Lie with me!" And he left his garment in her hand and fled, and went outside.

- Overview: Joseph's encounter with Potiphar's wife is one of the most direct examples of fleeing from sexual immorality. When faced with temptation, Joseph didn't try to reason with her or stay in a compromising situation. Instead, he literally ran away, prioritizing his integrity and commitment to God over any momentary desire or fear of consequences. His response shows the importance of immediate action to avoid sin.

### 2. JOB – SETTING BOUNDARIES TO AVOID TEMPTATION

- Scripture: Job 31:1
  "I have made a covenant with my eyes; how then could I gaze at a virgin?"

- Overview: Job demonstrated a proactive approach to purity by making a covenant with his eyes, committing not to gaze at women in a lustful way. This "covenant" was a personal boundary that kept his thoughts and desires in line with God's standards. By guarding his eyes and mind, Job exemplified the importance of setting boundaries to avoid temptation, even before it appears.

### 3. DAVID – A LESSON IN THE CONSEQUENCES OF NOT FLEEING

- Scripture: 2 Samuel 11:2-4
  "Now when evening came David arose from his bed and walked around on the roof of the king's house, and from the roof he saw a woman bathing; and the woman was very beautiful in appearance. So David sent and inquired about the woman… Then David sent messengers and took her, and when she came to him, he lay with her."

- Overview: While David did not flee from sexual temptation in this instance, his story serves as a powerful lesson about the consequences of failing to do so. His decision to remain in a tempting situation led to sin, guilt, and significant consequences for himself and his family. David's experience highlights the importance of fleeing from temptation to prevent destructive outcomes. Later, however, David repented deeply, showing the importance of seeking God's forgiveness when we fall.

**Callout:** *"The Bible doesn't tell us to fight sexual temptation; it tells us to flee. Sometimes the most courageous thing you can do is run from the thing that would destroy you."*— ***Tim Keller***

# LIVING IN HOLINESS AND HONOR

## WEEK 24: LIVING IN HOLINESS AND HONOR

As followers of Christ, we are called to live lives set apart, reflecting God's character and bringing honor to His name. Holiness isn't about striving for perfection on our own; it's about surrendering to God's work within us, allowing His Spirit to shape us to be more like Jesus. In 1 Thessalonians 4:7, Paul writes, *"For God has not called us for the purpose of impurity, but in sanctification."* Living in holiness and honor means walking in alignment with God's standards and treating ourselves and others with the respect and dignity that He commands.

Living a holy life is about more than avoiding sin; it's about actively pursuing righteousness, humility, and integrity. It involves making intentional choices that honor God in our thoughts, words, and actions. When we choose holiness, we are choosing to reflect God's love and purity to a world in need of hope and truth. This life of honor brings glory to God and creates a powerful testimony to those around us.

This week, we'll explore practical steps to live in holiness and honor, focusing on aligning our lives with God's purpose. Reflect on your own journey and ask yourself: Are my daily choices bringing honor to God? How can I pursue holiness in my relationships, work, and personal life? Remember, God has equipped you with everything you need to live a life that honors Him, and He is faithful to guide you every step of the way.

- Focus: Pursuing a lifestyle of purity and holiness before God.
- Key Scriptures: 1 Thessalonians 4:3-8, Matthew 5:27-28
- Discussion Questions:

1. What does it look like to live a life of purity and honor in today's world?

2. How does maintaining purity impact your relationships with God, your spouse (if applicable), and others?

- Action Step: Write a personal commitment to purity in thoughts, actions, and relationships. Share this commitment with an accountability partner for support.

- Man Up Challenge: Pray daily for the strength to honor God with your body and mind. Ask God to give you the grace to live out your commitment to purity, and continue to seek accountability in this area.

**Week 24 Bible Reading**: *1 Chronicles 16–29; Luke 15–16*

## Using the 22 Questions for Accountability

John Wesley and his Holy Club were renowned for their dedication to spiritual growth and rigorous accountability. At the heart of their gatherings were 22 questions that challenged each member to examine their faith, actions, and intentions. These questions were designed to help men remain focused on their walk with Christ, to grow in holiness, and to hold each other accountable to living out the Gospel daily.

In a world full of distractions and temptations, it's easy to drift in our spiritual lives without even realizing it. The 22 questions serve as a powerful tool to bring us back into alignment with God's will and to cultivate a life of intentional faith. They cover areas such as integrity, personal holiness, and commitment to spiritual disciplines, calling us to examine our hearts deeply and honestly.

Using these questions for accountability, whether in a group setting or personal reflection, can strengthen your walk with Christ by fostering humility, transparency, and a commitment to spiritual growth. As we go through these questions, consider how they apply to your life and how you can use them to grow as a man of God. True accountability isn't just about pointing out faults; it's about walking alongside one another, encouraging one another, and pushing one another toward holiness.

In your final week for this session, we encourage you to reflect on these questions with a trusted brother in Christ. Reflect and review the past four weeks and check your **prayer request** and the people you are praying for. Did you see God move? Allow these questions to challenge you to greater faithfulness, as they have for countless men of faith through the centuries.

1. Am I consciously or unconsciously creating the impression that I am better than I really am? In other words, am I a hypocrite?
2. Am I honest in all my acts and words, or do I exaggerate?
3. Do I confidentially pass on to another what was told to me in confidence?
4. Can I be trusted?
5. Am I a slave to dress, friends, work, or habits?
6. Am I self-conscious, self-pitying, or self-justifying?
7. Did the Bible live in me today?

8. Do I give it time to speak to me everyday?
9. Am I enjoying prayer?
10. When did I last speak to someone else about my faith?
11. Do I pray about the money I spend?
12. Do I get to bed on time and get up on time?
13. Do I disobey God in anything?
14. Do I insist upon doing something about which my conscience is uneasy?
15. Am I defeated in any part of my life?
16. Am I jealous, impure, critical, irritable, touchy, or distrustful?
17. How do I spend my spare time?
18. Am I proud?
19. Do I thank God that I am not as other people, especially as the Pharisees who despised the publican?
20. Is there anyone whom I fear, dislike, disown, criticize, hold a resentment toward or disregard? If so, what am I doing about it?
21. Do I grumble or complain constantly?
22. Is Christ real to me?

*Callout- "Living a life of holiness and honor isn't just about what you avoid; it's about what you pursue. When you choose to honor God in everything, you're making a statement that His ways are higher and His standards are worth following."*
***—Jody Burkeen***

# CHAPTER 7
# STEWARDSHIP OF TIME AND RESOURCES

# WHERE YOUR TREASURE IS

## WEEK 25: WHERE YOUR TREASURE IS

What we treasure reveals what truly matters to us. Jesus taught us that our hearts naturally follow what we value most, whether it's possessions, status, relationships, or God Himself. In Matthew 6:21, Jesus says, *"For where your treasure is, there your heart will be also."* This powerful statement challenges us to examine what we prioritize and invest in. Are we storing up treasures that fade away, or are we investing in what is eternal?

Living with the right priorities means recognizing that earthly treasures—money, success, and possessions—are temporary. While they may provide comfort or security for a moment, they cannot satisfy the deepest needs of our hearts or last beyond this life. God calls us to set our hearts on things above, to treasure our relationship with Him, and to invest in what brings lasting impact and eternal rewards.

This week, we'll reflect on where our treasures truly lie and consider how to align our hearts with God's values. Ask yourself: What am I truly seeking? Are my goals and desires focused on temporary gains or on things that have eternal significance? Remember, when we treasure God above all else, our lives become a reflection of His kingdom, and our hearts find true peace and fulfillment.

- Focus: Understanding the biblical view of storing up treasures in heaven.
- Key Scripture: Matthew 6:19-21

> *" 19 "Do not store up for yourselves treasures on earth, where moth and rust destroy, and where thieves break in and steal. 20 But store up for yourselves treasures in heaven, where neither moth nor rust destroys, and where thieves do not break in or steal; 21 for where your treasure is, there your heart will be also."*

- Discussion Questions:

1. What does it mean to store up treasures in heaven rather than on earth?

_______________________________________________

_______________________________________________

_______________________________________________

_______________________________________________

_______________________________________________

_______________________________________________

_______________________________________________

_______________________________________________

_______________________________________________

2. How do your current priorities reflect where your treasure is?

_______________________________________________

_______________________________________________

_______________________________________________

_______________________________________________

_______________________________________________

_______________________________________________

- Action Step: Take a personal inventory of how you currently spend your time and resources. Identify any areas where your focus may be on earthly treasures rather than heavenly ones. Someone once said, "Check your checkbook if you want to know where your heart is."

- Man Up Challenge: Commit to shifting one area of your life toward a more heavenly focus this week, whether through giving, serving, or prioritizing time with God.

**Week 25 Bible Reading**: *2 Chronicles 1–15; Luke 17–18*

**Week 25- Accountability Questions for You and/ or Your Group: (End each week, holding each other accountable with these questions. Be honest; this is where we grow.) You are halfway through this study. Don't let your answers become rote. Be open and honest where you really are spiritually.**

| | | Yes | No |
|---|---|---|---|
| 1. | Have you spent daily time in the Scriptures and in prayer? | | |
| 2. | Have you had any impure thoughts that would not glorify God? | | |
| 3. | Have you been completely above reproach in your financial dealings? | | |
| 4. | Have you spent quality relationship time with family and friends? | | |
| 5. | Have you done your 100% best in your job, school, home, etc.? | | |
| 6. | Have you told any half-truths or outright lies, putting yourself in a better light to those around you? | | |
| 7. | Have you shared the Gospel with an unbeliever this week? | | |
| 8. | Have you taken care of your body through daily physical exercise and proper eating/sleeping habits? | | |
| 9. | Have you allowed any person or circumstance to rob you of your joy? | | |
| 10. | Have you lied on any of your answers today? | | |

| **Prayer Request** | **Name 5 People To Pray for this Week** |
|---|---|
| • ______________________ | • ______________________ |
| • ______________________ | • ______________________ |
| • ______________________ | • ______________________ |
| • ______________________ | • ______________________ |
| • ______________________ | • ______________________ |
| • ______________________ | • ______________________ |
| • ______________________ | • ______________________ |

**Each week, we will give you men in the Bible who exemplified the main theme. Take time this week to study these men.**

**1. Abraham – Treasuring God's Promises Above Earthly Possessions**

- **Scripture:** Hebrews 11:9-10
  *"By faith he lived as an alien in the land of promise, as in a foreign land, dwelling in tents with Isaac and Jacob, fellow heirs of the same promise; for he was looking for the city which has foundations, whose architect and builder is God."*

- **Overview:** Abraham left his homeland and lived as a wanderer, prioritizing God's promises over earthly security and comfort. His treasure was not in material possessions or a permanent home but in the promises of God. Abraham's faith in God's future provision exemplifies a heart set on eternal values rather than temporary comforts.

**2. Moses – Choosing Eternal Rewards Over Temporary Pleasures**

- **Scripture:** Hebrews 11:24-26
  *"By faith Moses, when he had grown up, refused to be called the son of Pharaoh's daughter, choosing rather to endure ill-treatment with the people of God than to enjoy the passing pleasures of sin, considering the reproach of Christ greater riches than the treasures of Egypt; for he was looking to the reward."*

- **Overview:** Moses had access to all the wealth and privileges of Egypt but chose to identify with God's people and endure hardship. He valued the eternal reward of faithfulness to God over the temporary pleasures and treasures of Egypt, showing where his heart truly lay.

**3. Paul – Treasuring Christ Above All Earthly Gain**

- **Scripture:** Philippians 3:7-8
  *"But whatever things were gain to me, those things I have counted as loss for the sake of Christ. More than that, I count all things to be loss in view of the surpassing value of knowing Christ Jesus my Lord, for whom I have suffered the loss of all things, and count them but rubbish so that I may gain Christ."*

- **Overview:** Paul, once a prominent religious leader with status and accomplishments, willingly gave up everything for the sake of Christ. He viewed all his former achievements and possessions as worthless compared to the value of knowing and serving Jesus. Paul's life reflects a heart wholly devoted to God, with his treasure firmly set in Christ.

> *Callout- "When we make God our greatest treasure, we free ourselves from the grip of materialism and find our true security in Him. Earthly treasures fade, but the treasures we store up in heaven last forever."*— **Billy Graham**

# MAKING THE MOST OF YOUR TIME

## WEEK 26: MAKING THE MOST OF YOUR TIME

Time is one of the most precious resources God has given us, and unlike money or possessions, it's something we can never get back once it's gone. The Bible calls us to live intentionally, using our time wisely to honor God and fulfill His purposes. In Ephesians 5:15-16 (NASB), Paul urges, *"Therefore be careful how you walk, not as unwise men but as wise, making the most of your time, because the days are evil."* This reminder encourages us to evaluate how we spend our time and to prioritize what truly matters.

Making the most of our time means understanding that every day is an opportunity to serve God, grow in our faith, and positively impact others. This involves being intentional about setting goals, focusing on what aligns with God's will, and avoiding distractions that pull us away from our purpose. Time is a gift, and using it well allows us to live a life that's fulfilling, purposeful, and reflective of our commitment to Christ.

This week, we'll explore practical ways to make the most of the time God has given us. Reflect on your current routines and ask yourself: Am I using my time in a way that honors God? How can I be more intentional about the way I spend my days? Remember, every moment is an opportunity to live out your faith, serve others, and bring glory to God.

- **Focus:** Being wise in how you use your time for God's purposes.
- **Key Scripture:** Ephesians 5:15-17
  " 15 Therefore be careful how you walk, not as unwise men but as wise, 16 making
  the most of your time, because the days are evil. 17 So then do not be foolish,
  but understand what the will of the Lord is. ."
- **Discussion Questions:**

1. What does it mean to make the most of every opportunity?

_______________________________________________
_______________________________________________
_______________________________________________
_______________________________________________
_______________________________________________
_______________________________________________
_______________________________________________
_______________________________________________
_______________________________________________

2. How can you better prioritize your time for God's glory?

_______________________________________________
_______________________________________________
_______________________________________________
_______________________________________________
_______________________________________________
_______________________________________________
_______________________________________________
_______________________________________________
_______________________________________________

- **Action Step:** Create a daily or weekly schedule that prioritizes time for God (prayer, Bible reading, serving others), family, work, and rest.

- **Man Up Challenge:** Set aside at least 30 minutes each day this week for focused time with God. This could be in prayer, Bible study, or reflection on how to live wisely by God's will. If this is apart of your routine, find ways to add more time with God, family, and yourself.

**Week 26 Bible Reading**: *2 Chronicles 16–36; Luke 19–20*

**Week 26- Accountability Questions for You and/ or Your Group: (End each week, holding each other accountable with these questions. Be honest, this is where we grow.)**

| | | Yes | No |
|---|---|---|---|
| 1. | Have you spent daily time in the Scriptures and in prayer? | | |
| 2. | Have you had any impure thoughts that would not glorify God? | | |
| 3. | Have you been completely above reproach in your financial dealings? | | |
| 4. | Have you spent quality relationship time with family and friends? | | |
| 5. | Have you done your 100% best in your job, school, home, etc.? | | |
| 6. | Have you told any half-truths or outright lies, putting yourself in a better light to those around you? | | |
| 7. | Have you shared the Gospel with an unbeliever this week? | | |
| 8. | Have you taken care of your body through daily physical exercise and proper eating/sleeping habits? | | |
| 9. | Have you allowed any person or circumstance to rob you of your joy? | | |
| 10. | Have you lied on any of your answers today? | | |

| **Prayer Request** | **Name 5 People To Pray for this Week** |
|---|---|
| • ______________________ | • ______________________ |
| • ______________________ | • ______________________ |
| • ______________________ | • ______________________ |
| • ______________________ | • ______________________ |
| • ______________________ | • ______________________ |
| • ______________________ | • ______________________ |
| • ______________________ | • ______________________ |

**Each week, we will give you men in the Bible who exemplified the main theme. Take time this week to study these men.**

**1. Jesus – Prioritizing His Mission and Spending Time in Prayer**

- **Scripture:** Mark 1:35-38
  *"In the early morning, while it was still dark, Jesus got up, left the house, and went away to a secluded place, and was praying there. Simon and his companions searched for Him; they found Him and said to Him, 'Everyone is looking for You.' He said to them, 'Let us go somewhere else to the towns nearby, so that I may preach there also; for that is what I came for.'"*

- **Overview:** Jesus made the most of His time by focusing on His mission to preach, teach, and bring people closer to God. He also prioritized time in prayer, often withdrawing to pray and seek strength from the Father. Jesus exemplified intentionality by staying focused on God's purpose for His life, ensuring that every action aligned with His divine calling.

**2. Paul – Diligently Preaching the Gospel and Encouraging Believers**

- **Scripture:** Acts 20:24
  *"But I do not consider my life of any account as dear to myself, so that I may finish my course and the ministry which I received from the Lord Jesus, to testify solemnly of the gospel of the grace of God."*

- **Overview:** Paul's life was marked by a relentless dedication to spreading the Gospel and strengthening the early church. He traveled extensively, endured hardships, and devoted himself fully to the ministry God had given him. Paul exemplified making the most of his time by prioritizing God's work above all else, even when it required personal sacrifice.

**3. Nehemiah – Leading the Reconstruction of Jerusalem's Walls with Determination**

- **Scripture:** Nehemiah 6:3
  *"So I sent messengers to them, saying, 'I am doing a great work and I cannot come down. Why should the work stop while I leave it and come down to you?'"*

- **Overview:** Nehemiah displayed focus and determination as he led the rebuilding of Jerusalem's walls despite opposition and distractions. He understood the importance of his mission and refused to be sidetracked. Nehemiah made the most of his time by staying committed to the work God called him to, exemplifying persistence and purposefulness in fulfilling his duty.

> *"Time is one of the most valuable resources God gives us. Making the most of it means choosing purpose over distraction, letting God's priorities become our own, and using each moment to make a lasting impact."*— **Jody Burkeen**

# STEWARDSHIP OF YOUR RESOURCES

## WEEK 27: STEWARDSHIP OF YOUR RESOURCES

Everything we have—our finances, talents, time, and possessions—ultimately belongs to God, entrusted to us to manage wisely. Biblical stewardship is about recognizing that God is the true owner of all we possess and that we are called to use these resources in a way that honors Him and impacts His kingdom. In 1 Peter 4:10 (NASB), we are reminded, *"As each one has received a special gift, employ it in serving one another as good stewards of the manifold grace of God."* This call to stewardship goes beyond money; it encompasses all the gifts, opportunities, and resources we've been given.

Being a good steward means managing resources with purpose, generosity, and gratitude, using them to serve others and glorify God. Rather than storing up treasures for ourselves, we are to invest in things that have eternal value, such as helping those in need, supporting God's work, and using our talents to serve others. Stewardship is an expression of trust in God's provision and a commitment to reflect His generosity and grace.

This week, we'll explore practical ways to steward our resources faithfully, looking at how we can better align our finances, time, and talents with God's purpose. Reflect on how you are currently using what God has given you: Are you managing your resources in a way that honors Him? How can you better serve others with what you have? Remember, good stewardship is an act of worship, an opportunity to impact others, and a way to participate in God's work on earth.

- **Focus:** Managing your finances and resources as a steward of God's gifts.
- **Key Scripture:** 1 Timothy 6:17-19

> *"17 Instruct those who are rich in this present world not to be conceited or to fix their hope on the uncertainty of riches, but on God, who richly supplies us with all things to enjoy. 18 Instruct them to do good, to be rich in good works, to be generous and ready to share, 19 storing up for themselves the treasure of a good foundation for the future, so that they may take hold of that which is life indeed."*

- **Discussion Questions:**

1. How does trusting in God rather than wealth change the way you manage your finances?

_______________________________________________

_______________________________________________

_______________________________________________

_______________________________________________

_______________________________________________

_______________________________________________

_______________________________________________

2. In what ways can you be more generous with the resources God has entrusted to you?

_______________________________________________

_______________________________________________

_______________________________________________

_______________________________________________

_______________________________________________

_______________________________________________

_______________________________________________

- **Action Step:** Create a personal or family budget that reflects biblical stewardship. Prioritize tithing, giving, saving, and spending in ways that honor God. (insert link for budget help)

- **Man Up Challenge:** Tithe consistently this week if you aren't already, and seek opportunities to be generous with your resources. Reflect on how your budget can glorify God.

**Week 27 Bible Reading**: *Ezra 1–10; Nehemiah 1–7; Luke 21–22*

**Week 27- Accountability Questions for You and/ or Your Group: (End each week, holding each other accountable with these questions. Be honest, this is where we grow.)**

| | | Yes | No |
|---|---|---|---|
| 1. | Have you spent daily time in the Scriptures and in prayer? | | |
| 2. | Have you had any impure thoughts that would not glorify God? | | |
| 3. | Have you been completely above reproach in your financial dealings? | | |
| 4. | Have you spent quality relationship time with family and friends? | | |
| 5. | Have you done your 100% best in your job, school, home, etc.? | | |
| 6. | Have you told any half-truths or outright lies, putting yourself in a better light to those around you? | | |
| 7. | Have you shared the Gospel with an unbeliever this week? | | |
| 8. | Have you taken care of your body through daily physical exercise and proper eating/sleeping habits? | | |
| 9. | Have you allowed any person or circumstance to rob you of your joy? | | |
| 10. | Have you lied on any of your answers today? | | |

| **Prayer Request** | **Name 5 People To Pray for this Week** |
|---|---|
| • ______________________ | • ______________________ |
| • ______________________ | • ______________________ |
| • ______________________ | • ______________________ |
| • ______________________ | • ______________________ |
| • ______________________ | • ______________________ |
| • ______________________ | • ______________________ |
| • ______________________ | • ______________________ |

**Each week, we will give you men in the Bible who exemplified the main theme. Take time this week to study these men.**

1. **Joseph – Managing Resources for the Benefit of Others**

   - **Scripture:** Genesis 41:56-57
     *"When the famine was spread over all the face of the earth, then Joseph opened all the storehouses and sold to the Egyptians; and the famine was severe in the land of Egypt. The people of all the earth came to Egypt to buy grain from Joseph, because the famine was severe in all the earth."*

   - **Overview:** As a wise and faithful steward of Egypt's resources, Joseph used his position and God-given wisdom to store up grain during years of abundance. When famine struck, he managed these resources to provide for Egypt and surrounding nations. Joseph's example demonstrates stewardship that goes beyond personal gain, prioritizing the welfare of others and honoring God's guidance.

2. **Nehemiah – Stewarding Resources and Leadership to Rebuild**

   - **Scripture:** Nehemiah 2:8
     *"And a letter to Asaph the keeper of the king's forest, that he may give me timber to make beams for the gates of the fortress which is by the temple, for the wall of the city and for the house to which I will go. And the king granted them to me because the good hand of my God was on me."*

   - **Overview:** Nehemiah used his position, resources, and leadership skills to rebuild the walls of Jerusalem. He carefully allocated materials and led the people in the rebuilding efforts, showing stewardship not only of physical resources but also of his role as a leader. Nehemiah's commitment to using what was given to him for God's purpose is a model of dedicated stewardship.

3. **Solomon – Generous Stewardship in Building the Temple**

   - **Scripture:** 1 Kings 6:11-13
     *"Now the word of the Lord came to Solomon saying, 'Concerning this house which you are building, if you will walk in My statutes and execute My ordinances and keep all My commandments by walking in them, then I will carry out My word with you which I spoke to David your father. I will dwell among the sons of Israel and will not forsake My people Israel.'"*

- **Overview:** Solomon used the resources of his kingdom generously to build a temple for the Lord, sparing no expense to create a place of worship that would honor God. He understood that his wealth and wisdom were blessings from God and used them for God's glory. Solomon's careful, generous, and reverent use of resources demonstrates a heart of stewardship focused on honoring God.

> *"Stewardship is not just about managing your money; it's about managing your life for the glory of God. Every resource, every talent, every moment is a gift from Him, and true stewardship is using those gifts to honor His purpose.* — ***Randy Alcorn***

# USING YOUR TALENTS FOR GOD'S GLORY

## WEEK 28: USING YOUR TALENTS FOR GOD'S GLORY

Every talent, skill, and ability we possess is a gift from God, meant to serve others and bring glory to Him. The Bible reminds us in 1 Peter 4:10-11, "As each one has received a special gift, employ it in serving one another as good stewards of the manifold grace of God… so that in all things God may be glorified through Jesus Christ." God didn't give us our talents just for personal gain or recognition; He gave them so that we could make a meaningful impact in His kingdom.

Using our talents for God's glory means seeking opportunities to use our unique gifts to serve others, contribute to our communities, and advance the work of His church. It involves a mindset shift—from seeing talents as our own to viewing them as tools God entrusted to us for a greater purpose. When we use our gifts with humility and gratitude, we reflect God's creativity and love to those around us, making Him known through our actions.

This week, we'll explore what it looks like to use your talents for God's purposes, focusing on practical ways to serve and honor Him with the skills He has given you. Reflect on your own talents and ask yourself: Am I using my abilities in ways that bring glory to God? How can I use my gifts to serve others and further His kingdom? Remember, each talent you possess is an opportunity to shine God's light and make a difference.

- Focus: Discovering and using your talents and gifts in service to God.
- Key Scripture: 1 Peter 4:10

> *"10 As each one has received a special gift, employ it in serving one another as good stewards of the manifold grace of God."*

- Discussion Questions:

1. What gifts and talents has God given you to serve others?

2. How can you use these talents more intentionally in your church and community?

- Action Step: Identify your spiritual gifts or talents. Find a way to use these gifts in service to your local church or a ministry this week. (Insert Spiritual Gifts Test Website)

_______________________________________________

_______________________________________________

_______________________________________________

_______________________________________________

_______________________________________________

_______________________________________________

_______________________________________________

- Man Up Challenge: Commit to consistently serving in your local church or community. Seek out opportunities where your talents can make a difference in God's kingdom.

_______________________________________________

_______________________________________________

_______________________________________________

_______________________________________________

_______________________________________________

_______________________________________________

**Ongoing Application:**

- Daily Discipline: Continue managing your time, money, and talents to glorify God. Reassess your schedule and budget regularly to ensure they reflect godly priorities.
- Accountability: Share your stewardship journey with a trusted friend or group for encouragement and hold each other accountable for using your resources wisely.

**Week 28 Bible Reading**: *Nehemiah 8–13; Esther 1–10; Luke 23–24*

## Using the 22 Questions for Accountability

John Wesley and his Holy Club were renowned for their dedication to spiritual growth and rigorous accountability. At the heart of their gatherings were 22 questions that challenged each member to examine their faith, actions, and intentions. These questions were designed to help men remain focused on their walk with Christ, to grow in holiness, and to hold each other accountable to living out the Gospel daily.

In a world full of distractions and temptations, it's easy to drift in our spiritual lives without even realizing it. The 22 questions serve as a powerful tool to bring us back into alignment with God's will and to cultivate a life of intentional faith. They cover areas such as integrity, personal holiness, and commitment to spiritual disciplines, calling us to examine our hearts deeply and honestly.

Using these questions for accountability, whether in a group setting or personal reflection, can strengthen your walk with Christ by fostering humility, transparency, and a commitment to spiritual growth. As we go through these questions, consider how they apply to your life and how you can use them to grow as a man of God. True accountability isn't just about pointing out faults; it's about walking alongside one another, encouraging one another, and pushing one another toward holiness.

In your final week for this session, we encourage you to reflect on these questions with a trusted brother in Christ. Reflect and review the past four weeks and check your **prayer request** and the people you are praying for. Did you see God move? Allow these questions to challenge you to greater faithfulness, as they have for countless men of faith through the centuries.

1. Am I consciously or unconsciously creating the impression that I am better than I really am? In other words, am I a hypocrite?
2. Am I honest in all my acts and words, or do I exaggerate?
3. Do I confidentially pass on to another what was told to me in confidence?
4. Can I be trusted?
5. Am I a slave to dress, friends, work, or habits?
6. Am I self-conscious, self-pitying, or self-justifying?
7. Did the Bible live in me today?

8. Do I give it time to speak to me everyday?
9. Am I enjoying prayer?
10. When did I last speak to someone else about my faith?
11. Do I pray about the money I spend?
12. Do I get to bed on time and get up on time?
13. Do I disobey God in anything?
14. Do I insist upon doing something about which my conscience is uneasy?
15. Am I defeated in any part of my life?
16. Am I jealous, impure, critical, irritable, touchy, or distrustful?
17. How do I spend my spare time?
18. Am I proud?
19. Do I thank God that I am not as other people, especially as the Pharisees who despised the publican?
20. Is there anyone whom I fear, dislike, disown, criticize, hold a resentment toward or disregard? If so, what am I doing about it?
21. Do I grumble or complain constantly?
22. Is Christ real to me?

*Callout- "God gave you talents for a reason—not just to benefit yourself, but to make an impact for His Kingdom. When you use your gifts to serve others and point them to Christ, you're honoring the purpose He placed within you."—* ***Jody Burkeen***

# CHAPTER 8
# EVANGELISM AND DISCIPLESHIP

# THE GREAT COMMISSION

## WEEK 29: THE GREAT COMMISSION

Before Jesus ascended to heaven, He left His disciples with a powerful mission: to go and make disciples of all nations, spreading the message of salvation and sharing His love with the world. This mission, known as the Great Commission, is found in Matthew 28:18-20 *"And Jesus came up and spoke to them, saying, 'All authority has been given to Me in heaven and on earth. Go therefore and make disciples of all the nations, baptizing them in the name of the Father and the Son and the Holy Spirit, teaching them to observe all that I commanded you; and lo, I am with you always, even to the end of the age.'"* These words reveal the heart of Jesus' call for all believers—to take His message beyond our immediate surroundings and make His name known throughout the world.

The Great Commission is not just for pastors or missionaries; it's a call for every believer to participate in sharing the Gospel, making disciples, and living in a way that points others to Christ. It challenges us to step out of our comfort zones, engage with people who may not know God, and commit to helping them grow in faith. Whether through conversations, acts of service, or sharing our personal testimonies, each of us has a unique role in fulfilling this mission.

This week, we'll explore what it means to live out the Great Commission in our daily lives. Reflect on how you can be intentional about sharing God's love and truth with those around you. Ask yourself: Am I actively participating in Jesus' call to make disciples? How can I make an impact for His Kingdom right where I am? Remember, the Great Commission is a lifelong mission that brings purpose and fulfillment as we share the life-changing message of Jesus Christ.

- **Focus:** Understanding the call to evangelism and discipleship.
- **Key Scripture:** Matthew 28:18-20

> *"18 And Jesus came up and spoke to them, saying, "All authority has been given to Me in heaven and on earth. 19 Go therefore and make disciples of all the nations, baptizing them in the name of the Father and the Son and the Holy Spirit, 20 teaching them to observe all that I commanded you; and lo, I am with you always, even to the end of the age."""*

- **Discussion Questions:**

1. What does Jesus mean when He commands us to "make disciples"?

_______________________________________________

_______________________________________________

_______________________________________________

_______________________________________________

2. How can we actively engage in this mission today?

_______________________________________________

_______________________________________________

_______________________________________________

_______________________________________________

_______________________________________________

3. Name five men you could disciple

_______________________________________________

_______________________________________________

_______________________________________________

_______________________________________________

_______________________________________________

- **Action Step:** Reflect on your current involvement in evangelism and discipleship. Identify one person you can begin to disciple or share the Gospel with.

- **Man Up Challenge:** This week, commit to sharing the Great Commission with a fellow believer and discussing how you can work together to fulfill this calling.

**Week 29 Bible Reading**: *Job 1–21; John 1–2*

**Week 29- Accountability Questions for You and/ or Your Group: (End each week, holding each other accountable with these questions. Be honest, this is where we grow.)**

| | | Yes | No |
|---|---|---|---|
| 1. | Have you spent daily time in the Scriptures and in prayer? | | |
| 2. | Have you had any impure thoughts that would not glorify God? | | |
| 3. | Have you been completely above reproach in your financial dealings? | | |
| 4. | Have you spent quality relationship time with family and friends? | | |
| 5. | Have you done your 100% best in your job, school, home, etc.? | | |
| 6. | Have you told any half-truths or outright lies, putting yourself in a better light to those around you? | | |
| 7. | Have you shared the Gospel with an unbeliever this week? | | |
| 8. | Have you taken care of your body through daily physical exercise and proper eating/sleeping habits? | | |
| 9. | Have you allowed any person or circumstance to rob you of your joy? | | |
| 10. | Have you lied on any of your answers today? | | |

**Prayer Request**

- __________
- __________
- __________
- __________
- __________
- __________
- __________

**Name 5 People To Pray for this Week**

- __________
- __________
- __________
- __________
- __________
- __________
- __________

**Each week, we will give you men in the Bible who exemplified the main theme. Take time this week to study these men.**

**1. Peter – Boldly Preaching the Gospel to All Nations**

- Scripture: Acts 2:38-39
  "Peter said to them, 'Repent, and each of you be baptized in the name of Jesus Christ for the forgiveness of your sins; and you will receive the gift of the Holy Spirit. For the promise is for you and your children and for all who are far off, as many as the Lord our God will call to Himself.'"

- Overview: On the day of Pentecost, Peter stood up to preach to a diverse crowd, boldly proclaiming the Gospel and calling people to repentance and baptism. His message led to thousands of conversions and marked the beginning of the church. Peter's boldness and commitment to spreading the message to people from different nations show his dedication to the Great Commission.

**2. Philip – Sharing the Gospel with Individuals and Foreigners**

- Scripture: Acts 8:35
  "Then Philip opened his mouth, and beginning from this Scripture he preached Jesus to him."

- Overview: Philip's encounter with the Ethiopian eunuch illustrates the importance of personal evangelism. When God directed Philip to approach the Ethiopian's chariot, Philip explained the Scriptures and shared the Gospel, leading the man to faith and baptism. Philip's obedience to God's prompting shows that the Great Commission involves reaching out to individuals as well as crowds.

**3. Paul – Spreading the Gospel Across Regions and Establishing Churches**

- Scripture: Romans 15:20-21
  "And thus I aspired to preach the gospel, not where Christ was already named, so that I would not build on another man's foundation; but as it is written, 'They who had no news of Him shall see, and they who have not heard shall understand.'"

- Overview: Paul's life and ministry were dedicated to fulfilling the Great Commission. He traveled extensively, preaching the Gospel to Gentiles and Jews alike, establishing churches, and writing letters to encourage believers. Paul's passion for reaching those who hadn't heard of Christ and his commitment to planting churches exemplify the Great Commission in action.

> *"The Great Commission is not a suggestion to be considered; it's a command to be obeyed. We are called to go, not to stay, and to share the love and truth of Christ with everyone, everywhere."*— ***Hudson Taylor***

# BE READY TO GIVE AN ANSWER

## WEEK 30: BE READY TO GIVE AN ANSWER

As followers of Christ, we are called to live with hope, and our lives should spark curiosity in those around us. When people see something different in us, they may ask questions about our faith, values, or the peace we have in difficult times. In 1 Peter 3:15 , we're reminded, "But sanctify Christ as Lord in your hearts, always being ready to make a defense to everyone who asks you to give an account for the hope that is in you, yet with gentleness and reverence." This verse calls us to be prepared to share our faith with clarity, respect, and humility, ready to explain the hope we have in Christ.

Being ready to give an answer means knowing what you believe and why you believe it. It involves understanding the foundation of your faith and being willing to share your personal testimony and the truth of the Gospel when opportunities arise. Preparation is key—spending time in God's Word, growing in understanding, and praying for the Holy Spirit's guidance help us respond with confidence and love when others inquire about our faith.

This week, we'll focus on what it means to be prepared to give an answer, looking at practical ways to articulate our faith effectively and respectfully. Reflect on your own readiness: Are you prepared to share your faith when someone asks? What steps can you take to grow in confidence and understanding? Remember, God equips us to be His witnesses, empowering us to share His love and truth with a world in need.

- Focus: Preparing to share your faith with confidence.
- Key Scripture: 1 Peter 3:15

> *"15 but sanctify Christ as Lord in your hearts, always being ready to make a defense to everyone who asks you to give an account for the hope that is in you, yet with gentleness and reverence;"*

- Discussion Questions:

1. What does it mean to always be prepared to share your faith?

   ______________________________________________

   ______________________________________________

   ______________________________________________

   ______________________________________________

   ______________________________________________

2. How can you communicate the Gospel with gentleness and respect?

   ______________________________________________

   ______________________________________________

   ______________________________________________

   ______________________________________________

3. Look around at the people in your sphere of influence. Who has God sent so they can hear the gospel? List those people below:

   ______________________________________________

   ______________________________________________

   ______________________________________________

   ______________________________________________

   ______________________________________________

- Action Step: Write down your personal testimony, focusing on how Christ has changed your life. Practice sharing it with a trusted friend or accountability partner. My Book Man Up- Becoming a Godly Man in an Ungodly World was the end result of writing my testimony down.

- Man Up Challenge: Share your testimony with at least one person this week, whether it's a friend, family member, or co-worker. Be prepared to answer their questions with love and respect.

**Week 30 Bible Reading**: *Job 22–42; John 3–4*

**Week 30- Accountability Questions for You and/ or Your Group: (End each week, holding each other accountable with these questions. Be honest, this is where we grow.)**

| | | Yes | No |
|---|---|---|---|
| 1. | Have you spent daily time in the Scriptures and in prayer? | | |
| 2. | Have you had any impure thoughts that would not glorify God? | | |
| 3. | Have you been completely above reproach in your financial dealings? | | |
| 4. | Have you spent quality relationship time with family and friends? | | |
| 5. | Have you done your 100% best in your job, school, home, etc.? | | |
| 6. | Have you told any half-truths or outright lies, putting yourself in a better light to those around you? | | |
| 7. | Have you shared the Gospel with an unbeliever this week? | | |
| 8. | Have you taken care of your body through daily physical exercise and proper eating/sleeping habits? | | |
| 9. | Have you allowed any person or circumstance to rob you of your joy? | | |
| 10. | Have you lied on any of your answers today? | | |

**Prayer Request**

- ____________________
- ____________________
- ____________________
- ____________________
- ____________________
- ____________________
- ____________________

**Name 5 People To Pray for this Week**

- ____________________
- ____________________
- ____________________
- ____________________
- ____________________
- ____________________
- ____________________

**Each week, we will give you men in the Bible who exemplified the main theme. Take time this week to study these men.**

**1. Stephen – Boldly Defending His Faith in Front of the Sanhedrin**

- Scripture: Acts 7:51-52 (
  "You men who are stiff-necked and uncircumcised in heart and ears are always resisting the Holy Spirit; you are doing just as your fathers did. Which one of the prophets did your fathers not persecute?"

- Overview: When Stephen was brought before the Sanhedrin, he gave a powerful account of his faith, retelling Israel's history and how it pointed to Jesus as the Messiah. His deep understanding of Scripture allowed him to boldly defend his faith, even knowing it would likely cost him his life. Stephen's example shows a readiness to speak the truth, grounded in knowledge and conviction.

**2. Peter – Explaining the Gospel to a Diverse Crowd at Pentecost**

- Scripture: Acts 2:38-39
  "Peter said to them, 'Repent, and each of you be baptized in the name of Jesus Christ for the forgiveness of your sins; and you will receive the gift of the Holy Spirit. For the promise is for you and your children and for all who are far off, as many as the Lord our God will call to Himself.'"

- Overview: On the day of Pentecost, Peter addressed a large and diverse crowd, explaining the significance of Jesus' life, death, and resurrection. His message led to the conversion of thousands. Peter's readiness to answer questions about the Gospel and his courage to speak publicly show his commitment to sharing the hope of Christ with anyone who would listen.

**3. Paul – Reasoning with the Greeks at the Areopagus**

- Scripture: Acts 17:22-23
  "So Paul stood in the midst of the Areopagus and said, 'Men of Athens, I observe that you are very religious in all respects. For while I was passing through and examining the objects of your worship, I also found an altar with this inscription, "TO AN UNKNOWN GOD." Therefore what you worship in ignorance, this I proclaim to you.'"

- Overview: Paul's speech at the Areopagus in Athens shows his readiness to engage with people of different beliefs. He observed their culture and used it as a starting point to introduce them to the true God. Paul's ability to relate the Gospel to his audience's worldview exemplifies a thoughtful and prepared approach to sharing his faith in a way that connected with them.

> *"Being ready to give an answer means knowing why you believe and having the courage to speak it. Your faith is your story, and God has equipped you to share it with boldness and love."*— **Jody Burkeen**

# TEACHING AND DISCIPLING OTHERS

## WEEK 31: TEACHING AND DISCIPLING OTHERS

Jesus' final instructions to His followers were to go and make disciples of all nations, teaching them to obey everything He had commanded (Matthew 28:19-20 NASB). This call to disciple others is more than just sharing information; it's about investing in others' spiritual growth, guiding them in their walk with God, and modeling a life of faith. Discipleship involves building relationships, teaching biblical truth, and walking alongside others as they grow closer to Christ.

Teaching and discipling others requires humility, patience, and a commitment to living out the Gospel in daily life. It's not about having all the answers, but about being willing to share what God has taught you and helping others apply His Word to their lives. True discipleship creates lasting impact, as each generation of believers is equipped to disciple others, continuing the legacy of faith.

This week, we'll explore practical ways to teach and disciple others, focusing on building relationships, sharing biblical truth, and living as examples of Christ. Reflect on those in your life who may benefit from your guidance and support. Are you willing to step into a role of mentorship and encouragement? Remember, God has equipped you to make a difference in others' lives, and your investment in them can lead to a ripple effect of faith and growth.

- Focus: The role of teaching and investing in others through discipleship.
- Key Scripture: 2 Timothy 2:2

> *"2 The things which you have heard from me in the presence of many witnesses, entrust these to faithful men who will be able to teach others also."*

- Discussion Questions:

1. What does it mean to disciple someone and help them grow in their faith?

2. How can you find "reliable people" to disciple and mentor in the faith?

- Action Step: Identify someone in your life who is spiritually hungry and ready to grow. Begin meeting regularly to encourage and disciple them in their walk with Christ. List at five people who you think are ready:

- Man Up Challenge: Commit to mentoring at least one person this week. Set a time to meet, pray together, and start sharing biblical truths that will help them grow in their faith.

**Week 31**: *Psalms 1–37; John 5–6*

**Week 31- Accountability Questions for You and/ or Your Group: (End each week, holding each other accountable with these questions. Be honest, this is where we grow.)**

| | | Yes | No |
|---|---|---|---|
| 1. | Have you spent daily time in the Scriptures and in prayer? | | |
| 2. | Have you had any impure thoughts that would not glorify God? | | |
| 3. | Have you been completely above reproach in your financial dealings? | | |
| 4. | Have you spent quality relationship time with family and friends? | | |
| 5. | Have you done your 100% best in your job, school, home, etc.? | | |
| 6. | Have you told any half-truths or outright lies, putting yourself in a better light to those around you? | | |
| 7. | Have you shared the Gospel with an unbeliever this week? | | |
| 8. | Have you taken care of your body through daily physical exercise and proper eating/sleeping habits? | | |
| 9. | Have you allowed any person or circumstance to rob you of your joy? | | |
| 10. | Have you lied on any of your answers today? | | |

| **Prayer Request** | **Name 5 People To Pray for this Week** |
|---|---|
| • ______________________ | • ______________________ |
| • ______________________ | • ______________________ |
| • ______________________ | • ______________________ |
| • ______________________ | • ______________________ |
| • ______________________ | • ______________________ |
| • ______________________ | • ______________________ |
| • ______________________ | • ______________________ |

**Each week, we will give you men in the Bible who exemplified the main theme. Take time this week to study these men.**

**1. Jesus – The Ultimate Teacher and Discipler**

- **Scripture:** Matthew 4:19
  *"And He said to them, 'Follow Me, and I will make you fishers of men.'"*

- **Overview:** Jesus devoted His ministry to teaching and discipling others, particularly His twelve disciples. He spent time with them, taught them through parables, demonstrated God's love, and prepared them to carry on His mission. Jesus' approach to discipleship involved living alongside His followers, guiding them daily, and equipping them to become leaders in their own right.

**2. Paul – Mentoring Young Believers and Church Leaders**

- **Scripture:** 2 Timothy 2:2
  *"The things which you have heard from me in the presence of many witnesses, entrust these to faithful men who will be able to teach others also."*

- **Overview:** Paul exemplified teaching and discipleship through his letters, travels, and personal mentoring relationships. He discipled many young believers, including Timothy, whom he mentored as a spiritual son and church leader. Paul's commitment to teaching others who could then pass on their faith shows his dedication to multiplying disciples and strengthening the church.

**3. Barnabas – Encouraging and Supporting New Believers**

- **Scripture:** Acts 11:25-26 (NASB)
  *"And he left for Tarsus to look for Saul; and when he had found him, he brought him to Antioch. And for an entire year they met with the church and taught considerable numbers; and the disciples were first called Christians in Antioch."*

- **Overview:** Barnabas was known for his gift of encouragement and his willingness to invest in others. He played a key role in Paul's early ministry, mentoring him and bringing him to Antioch to teach new believers. Barnabas's example shows that discipleship often involves encouragement, support, and a commitment to helping others grow in faith.

*- "True discipleship is more than teaching; it's living out the Gospel alongside others, walking with them through their journey of faith, and helping them grow closer to Christ."*— **Dietrich Bonhoeffer**

# LIVING OUT THE GOSPEL DAILY

## WEEK 32: LIVING OUT THE GOSPEL DAILY

The Gospel isn't just a message to be heard on Sundays; it's a way of life that should impact every thought, action, and decision we make. To live out the Gospel daily means embodying the love, grace, and truth of Jesus in everything we do, reflecting His character to those around us. Jesus calls us not only to believe in Him but to follow Him, allowing the Gospel to shape our lives from the inside out. In Matthew 5:16 (NASB), Jesus says, *"Let your light shine before men in such a way that they may see your good works, and glorify your Father who is in heaven."*

Living out the Gospel daily involves surrendering our own desires, forgiving others as we have been forgiven, and showing compassion to those in need. It's about letting God's love transform us and spill over into our relationships, work, and interactions with others. This way of life challenges us to be intentional, to choose humility over pride, and to prioritize God's will above our own.

This week, we'll explore what it looks like to embody the Gospel each day. Reflect on areas in your life where you can better reflect Christ. Are there ways you can show more love, patience, or forgiveness? How can you let God's light shine through you in everyday situations? Remember, when we live out the Gospel daily, we become living testimonies of God's grace and love, drawing others closer to Him.

- Focus: Integrating evangelism and discipleship into your everyday life.
- Key Scriptures: Matthew 28:18-20, 1 Peter 3:15
- Discussion Questions:

1. How can you incorporate sharing the Gospel and discipling others into your daily routine?

    ______________________________________________________________________
    ______________________________________________________________________
    ______________________________________________________________________
    ______________________________________________________________________
    ______________________________________________________________________
    ______________________________________________________________________
    ______________________________________________________________________
    ______________________________________________________________________
    ______________________________________________________________________
    ______________________________________________________________________

2. What practical steps can you take to be more intentional about fulfilling the Great Commission?

    ______________________________________________________________________
    ______________________________________________________________________
    ______________________________________________________________________
    ______________________________________________________________________
    ______________________________________________________________________
    ______________________________________________________________________
    ______________________________________________________________________
    ______________________________________________________________________

- Action Step: Make a plan for how you can continue to engage in evangelism and discipleship beyond this study. This could include setting up regular meetings with those you are discipling, identifying more people to share the Gospel with, or joining an outreach ministry.

- Man Up Challenge: Make evangelism and discipleship a lifestyle by committing to ongoing conversations about Christ with those in your circles. Set goals for how you will continue this mission over the coming months.

### Ongoing Application:

- Daily Discipline: Continue sharing your testimony, studying Scripture with those you are discipling, and always being ready to share the Gospel with gentleness and respect.

#### 1. SET UP REGULAR MEETINGS WITH THOSE YOU ARE DISCIPLING

**Weekly or Bi-Weekly Check-ins**: Schedule regular times to meet with those you are currently discipling. These meetings can be in person or virtual, depending on what works best.

**Focus Topics**: Each meeting could cover a different topic, such as spiritual growth, prayer, specific Bible passages, or any challenges they're facing in their faith journey.

**Accountability and Support**: Use these times to encourage and hold each other accountable, helping each person grow in their relationship with Christ.

#### 2. IDENTIFY NEW PEOPLE TO SHARE THE GOSPEL WITH

**Pray for Opportunities**: Begin by asking God to open your eyes to people in your life who may be receptive to the Gospel. This could include friends, coworkers, family members, or acquaintances.

**Look for Natural Opportunities**: Be mindful of moments when people around you express a need or question that opens the door for spiritual conversation.

**Initiate Meaningful Conversations**: Use questions or statements that can gently guide discussions toward faith topics, and be prepared to share your personal testimony and the hope you have in Christ.

#### 3. JOIN OR START AN OUTREACH MINISTRY

**Local Church Ministry**: Consider joining an evangelism or discipleship ministry at your church. Many churches offer programs like community outreach, small groups, and missions that provide structured opportunities for sharing the Gospel.

**Community Service**: Find ways to serve your community, such as volunteering at shelters, food banks, or community events. Use these opportunities to meet new people and share the love of Christ through both words and actions.

**Start a Small Group**: If there isn't an outreach or discipleship ministry available, consider starting a small group in your home or community. Focus on studying the Bible and building a supportive, faith-centered community.

### 4. COMMIT TO ONGOING PERSONAL GROWTH

**Continue Learning**: Engage in regular Bible study and prayer to deepen your own faith. The stronger your relationship with God, the more prepared you'll be to disciple others.

**Read Books on Evangelism and Discipleship**: Resources from respected Christian authors can offer practical guidance on effective evangelism and discipleship strategies.

**Stay Accountable**: Find a mentor or accountability partner who can encourage and support you as you continue to engage in evangelism and discipleship.

### 5. MAKE A PLAN FOR LONG-TERM IMPACT

**Set Monthly Goals**: Establish achievable goals for sharing the Gospel or meeting with those you're discipling each month.

**Evaluate and Adjust**: Periodically assess your progress and be open to making adjustments. Evangelism and discipleship require flexibility as you respond to each person's unique needs and circumstances.

**Pray for Impact**: Continually ask God to use your efforts for His glory and to multiply the fruit of your work. Remember that discipleship is a lifelong commitment to investing in others and expanding God's kingdom.

By setting regular meetings, identifying new opportunities, joining or creating a ministry, committing to personal growth, and planning for long-term impact, you can continue to fulfill the call to evangelism and discipleship beyond this study. Remember, God equips and empowers you as you step out in faith to share His love and truth with others.

- **Accountability**: Share your discipleship journey and plan with others in your church or men's group for encouragement, and ask for feedback on how you can improve in both evangelism and discipleship.

**Week 32 Bible Reading**: *Psalms 38–75; John 7–8*

## Using the 22 Questions for Accountability

John Wesley and his Holy Club were renowned for their dedication to spiritual growth and rigorous accountability. At the heart of their gatherings were 22 questions that challenged each member to examine their faith, actions, and intentions. These questions were designed to help men remain focused on their walk with Christ, to grow in holiness, and to hold each other accountable to living out the Gospel daily.

In a world full of distractions and temptations, it's easy to drift in our spiritual lives without even realizing it. The 22 questions serve as a powerful tool to bring us back into alignment with God's will and to cultivate a life of intentional faith. They cover areas such as integrity, personal holiness, and commitment to spiritual disciplines, calling us to examine our hearts deeply and honestly.

Using these questions for accountability, whether in a group setting or personal reflection, can strengthen your walk with Christ by fostering humility, transparency, and a commitment to spiritual growth. As we go through these questions, consider how they apply to your life and how you can use them to grow as a man of God. True accountability isn't just about pointing out faults; it's about walking alongside one another, encouraging one another, and pushing one another toward holiness.

In your final week for this session, we encourage you to reflect on these questions with a trusted brother in Christ. Reflect and review the past four weeks and check your **prayer request** and the people you are praying for. Did you see God move? Allow these questions to challenge you to greater faithfulness, as they have for countless men of faith through the centuries.

1. Am I consciously or unconsciously creating the impression that I am better than I really am? In other words, am I a hypocrite?
2. Am I honest in all my acts and words, or do I exaggerate?
3. Do I confidentially pass on to another what was told to me in confidence?
4. Can I be trusted?
5. Am I a slave to dress, friends, work, or habits?
6. Am I self-conscious, self-pitying, or self-justifying?
7. Did the Bible live in me today?

8. Do I give it time to speak to me everyday?
9. Am I enjoying prayer?
10. When did I last speak to someone else about my faith?
11. Do I pray about the money I spend?
12. Do I get to bed on time and get up on time?
13. Do I disobey God in anything?
14. Do I insist upon doing something about which my conscience is uneasy?
15. Am I defeated in any part of my life?
16. Am I jealous, impure, critical, irritable, touchy, or distrustful?
17. How do I spend my spare time?
18. Am I proud?
19. Do I thank God that I am not as other people, especially as the Pharisees who despised the publican?
20. Is there anyone whom I fear, dislike, disown, criticize, hold a resentment toward or disregard? If so, what am I doing about it?
21. Do I grumble or complain constantly?
22. Is Christ real to me?

*Callout- "Living out the Gospel daily means letting your actions reflect Christ in everything you do. It's not just about what you say on Sunday; it's about how you live every day. Let your life be a testimony that points others to Jesus."*— ***Jody Burkeen***

# CHAPTER 9

# SPIRITUAL WARFARE

# UNDERSTANDING SPIRITUAL WARFARE

## WEEK 33: UNDERSTANDING SPIRITUAL WARFARE

The Christian life is not a life free from challenges or opposition; rather, it's a battleground where spiritual forces of good and evil are at work. Spiritual warfare is the struggle between God's truth and the deception of the enemy, between living for God and succumbing to temptation. The Bible reminds us in Ephesians 6:12, "For our struggle is not against flesh and blood, but against the rulers, against the powers, against the world forces of this darkness, against the spiritual forces of wickedness in the heavenly places." Understanding spiritual warfare means recognizing that we are in a constant, unseen battle and that our victory depends on God's strength and the spiritual armor He provides.

To navigate this battle, we need to be vigilant, equipped, and aware of the enemy's tactics. Satan seeks to undermine our faith, weaken our resolve, and distract us from God's purpose. But God has given us tools to stand firm—His Word, prayer, the shield of faith, and the support of fellow believers. Understanding spiritual warfare means knowing that we are not fighting alone and that our power comes from God, who has already claimed victory over the enemy through Jesus Christ.

This week, we will explore what it means to engage in spiritual warfare, how to identify the enemy's tactics, and the ways we can stand strong in God's power. Reflect on your own life: Are there areas where you feel under attack or discouraged? How can you strengthen your defenses through faith, prayer, and the Word? Remember, God is with you, equipping you for victory in every battle.

- Focus: Recognizing the reality of spiritual warfare.
- Key Scripture: 2 Corinthians 10:3-5

> *"3 For though we walk in the flesh, we do not war according to the flesh, 4 for the weapons of our warfare are not of the flesh, but divinely powerful for the destruction of fortresses. 5 We are destroying speculations and every lofty thing raised up against the knowledge of God, and we are taking every thought captive to the obedience of Christ,"*

- Discussion Questions:

1. What are the differences between worldly and spiritual battles?

2. What strongholds in your life need to be demolished through God's power?

- Action Step: Reflect on areas in your life where you are experiencing spiritual battles (e.g., doubts, temptations, or challenges). Write down specific strongholds that need to be broken in the power of Christ.

- Man Up Challenge: Begin each day this week by praying for God's strength to demolish the strongholds in your life. Ask Him to help you take captive every thought and make it obedient to Christ.

**Week 33 Bible Reading**: *Psalms 76–118; John 9–10*

**Week 33- Accountability Questions for You and/ or Your Group: (End each week, holding each other accountable with these questions. Be honest, this is where we grow.)**

| | | Yes | No |
|---|---|---|---|
| 1. | Have you spent daily time in the Scriptures and in prayer? | | |
| 2. | Have you had any impure thoughts that would not glorify God? | | |
| 3. | Have you been completely above reproach in your financial dealings? | | |
| 4. | Have you spent quality relationship time with family and friends? | | |
| 5. | Have you done your 100% best in your job, school, home, etc.? | | |
| 6. | Have you told any half-truths or outright lies, putting yourself in a better light to those around you? | | |
| 7. | Have you shared the Gospel with an unbeliever this week? | | |
| 8. | Have you taken care of your body through daily physical exercise and proper eating/sleeping habits? | | |
| 9. | Have you allowed any person or circumstance to rob you of your joy? | | |
| 10. | Have you lied on any of your answers today? | | |

**Prayer Request**

- __________
- __________
- __________
- __________
- __________
- __________
- __________

**Name 5 People To Pray for this Week**

- __________
- __________
- __________
- __________
- __________
- __________
- __________

**Each week, we will give you men in the Bible who exemplified the main theme. Take time this week to study these men.**

**1. Jesus – The Ultimate Teacher and Discipler**

- **Scripture:** Matthew 4:19
  *"And He said to them, 'Follow Me, and I will make you fishers of men.'"*

- **Overview:** Jesus devoted His ministry to teaching and discipling others, particularly His twelve disciples. He spent time with them, taught them through parables, demonstrated God's love, and prepared them to carry on His mission. Jesus' approach to discipleship involved living alongside His followers, guiding them daily, and equipping them to become leaders in their own right.

**2. Paul – Mentoring Young Believers and Church Leaders**

- **Scripture:** 2 Timothy 2:2
  *"The things which you have heard from me in the presence of many witnesses, entrust these to faithful men who will be able to teach others also."*

- **Overview:** Paul exemplified teaching and discipleship through his letters, travels, and personal mentoring relationships. He discipled many young believers, including Timothy, whom he mentored as a spiritual son and church leader. Paul's commitment to teaching others who could then pass on their faith shows his dedication to multiplying disciples and strengthening the church.

**3. Barnabas – Encouraging and Supporting New Believers**

- **Scripture:** Acts 11:25-26 (NASB)
  *"And he left for Tarsus to look for Saul; and when he had found him, he brought him to Antioch. And for an entire year they met with the church and taught considerable numbers; and the disciples were first called Christians in Antioch."*

- **Overview:** Barnabas was known for his gift of encouragement and his willingness to invest in others. He played a key role in Paul's early ministry, mentoring him and bringing him to Antioch to teach new believers. Barnabas's example shows that discipleship often involves encouragement, support, and a commitment to helping others grow in faith.

*Callout- "True discipleship is more than teaching; it's living out the Gospel alongside others, walking with them through their journey of faith, and helping them grow closer to Christ."*— **Dietrich Bonhoeffer**

# THE ARMOR OF GOD (PART 1)

## WEEK 34: THE ARMOR OF GOD (PART 1)

Life as a follower of Christ is not without its battles. As believers, we face spiritual challenges daily, from temptations to trials, all designed to weaken our faith and distract us from God's purpose. However, God has not left us defenseless. In Ephesians 6:10-11, Paul writes, *"Finally, be strong in the Lord and in the strength of His might. Put on the full armor of God, so that you will be able to stand firm against the schemes of the devil."* This armor equips us to face life's battles with confidence, ensuring that we stand firm in God's strength, not our own.

The armor of God isn't just a symbolic concept—it's a spiritual reality that protects, empowers, and equips us for daily life. Each piece of the armor—truth, righteousness, faith, and more—serves a specific purpose in guarding us against the enemy's attacks and enabling us to walk in victory. Understanding and putting on this armor is essential for standing firm in the face of spiritual warfare.

This week, we'll begin by exploring the first elements of the armor of God, focusing on how to apply them practically in your daily life. Reflect on areas where you feel spiritually vulnerable and ask yourself: Am I fully equipped with the armor God provides? How can I intentionally rely on His strength and truth? Remember, God has given you all the tools you need to stand strong, no matter what comes your way.

- Focus: Understanding and putting on the armor of God.
- Key Scripture: Ephesians 6:10-13

> *"10 Finally, be strong in the Lord and in the strength of His might. 11 Put on the full armor of God, so that you will be able to stand firm against the schemes of the devil. 12 For our struggle is not against flesh and blood, but against the rulers, against the powers, against the world forces of this darkness, against the spiritual forces of wickedness in the heavenly places. 13 Therefore, take up the full armor of God, so that you will be able to resist in the evil day, and having done everything, to stand firm. "*

- Discussion Questions:

1. Why is it important to put on the full armor of God?

______________________________________________

______________________________________________

______________________________________________

______________________________________________

______________________________________________

______________________________________________

2. How does knowing the nature of our spiritual enemy help us prepare for battle?

______________________________________________

______________________________________________

______________________________________________

______________________________________________

______________________________________________

______________________________________________

______________________________________________

- Action Step: Study the first three pieces of the armor of God: the belt of truth, the breastplate of righteousness, and the shoes of the gospel of peace (Ephesians 6:14-15). Identify how each piece can be applied to your life.

- The Belt of Truth:

1. The Breast Plate of Righteousness:

2. Shoes of the Gospel Peace:

- Man Up Challenge: Pray each morning this week, asking God to equip you with the belt of truth, the breastplate of righteousness, and the shoes of peace. Be mindful of how these spiritual tools protect and strengthen you throughout the day.

**Week 34 Bible Reading**: *Psalms 119–150; John 11–12*

**Week 34- Accountability Questions for You and/ or Your Group: (End each week, holding each other accountable with these questions. Be honest, this is where we grow.)**

| | | Yes | No |
|---|---|---|---|
| 1. | Have you spent daily time in the Scriptures and in prayer? | | |
| 2. | Have you had any impure thoughts that would not glorify God? | | |
| 3. | Have you been completely above reproach in your financial dealings? | | |
| 4. | Have you spent quality relationship time with family and friends? | | |
| 5. | Have you done your 100% best in your job, school, home, etc.? | | |
| 6. | Have you told any half-truths or outright lies, putting yourself in a better light to those around you? | | |
| 7. | Have you shared the Gospel with an unbeliever this week? | | |
| 8. | Have you taken care of your body through daily physical exercise and proper eating/sleeping habits? | | |
| 9. | Have you allowed any person or circumstance to rob you of your joy? | | |
| 10. | Have you lied on any of your answers today? | | |

**Prayer Request**

- ____________________
- ____________________
- ____________________
- ____________________
- ____________________
- ____________________
- ____________________

**Name 5 People To Pray for this Week**

- ____________________
- ____________________
- ____________________
- ____________________
- ____________________
- ____________________
- ____________________

**Each week, we will give you men in the Bible who exemplified the main theme. Take time this week to study these men.**

### 1. DAVID – TRUSTING IN GOD'S PROTECTION RATHER THAN PHYSICAL ARMOR

- Scripture: 1 Samuel 17:38-39
  "Then Saul clothed David with his garments and put a bronze helmet on his head, and he clothed him with armor. David girded his sword over his armor and tried to walk, for he had not tested them. So David said to Saul, 'I cannot go with these, for I have not tested them.' And David took them off."

- Overview: When David faced Goliath, he chose to rely on God's protection and strength rather than physical armor. Although Saul offered him traditional armor, David understood that his real defense was in his faith in God. By going into battle "armed" with faith, truth, and righteousness, David demonstrated reliance on spiritual armor over earthly means.

### 2. PAUL – LIVING OUT THE ARMOR OF GOD IN HIS MINISTRY

- Scripture: Acts 20:22-24
  "And now, behold, bound by the Spirit, I am on my way to Jerusalem, not knowing what will happen to me there, except that the Holy Spirit solemnly testifies to me in every city, saying that bonds and afflictions await me. But I do not consider my life of any account as dear to myself, so that I may finish my course and the ministry which I received from the Lord Jesus."

- Overview: Paul exemplified the armor of God through his life and ministry. His commitment to truth, his righteousness in Christ, and his unwavering faith allowed him to withstand persecution, imprisonment, and hardship. Paul's confidence in God's salvation and the power of prayer empowered him to continue his mission despite the dangers, embodying the armor of God he later described in Ephesians 6.

### 3. JOB – STANDING FIRM IN FAITH AMID SPIRITUAL ATTACK

- Scripture: Job 1:21-22
  "He said, 'Naked I came from my mother's womb, and naked I shall return there. The Lord gave and the Lord has taken away. Blessed be the name of the Lord.' Through all this Job did not sin nor did he blame God."

- Overview: Job's life exemplifies standing firm in faith during intense spiritual attack. Despite losing his health, family, and possessions, Job held onto his faith and integrity, demonstrating the "shield of faith" and the "helmet of salvation." His resistance against despair and anger illustrates a deep reliance on God's truth and righteousness, even in the face of adversity and temptation to doubt.

> *"The armor of God isn't just something you put on for the tough days; it's what you wear every day to live victoriously. Each piece reminds us that our strength comes from God and that He has equipped us to stand firm, no matter what comes our way."*
>
> **— Jody Burkeen**

# THE ARMOR OF GOD (PART 2)

## WEEK 35: THE ARMOR OF GOD (PART 2)

As believers, we are engaged in a spiritual battle that requires daily preparation and reliance on God's strength. The armor of God, described in Ephesians 6, is a powerful set of spiritual tools designed to protect us, strengthen our faith, and enable us to stand firm against the enemy's attacks. In Part 1, we explored some of the key pieces of this armor; in Part 2, we will continue examining how each element equips us to face spiritual warfare with confidence and victory.

The armor of God isn't physical gear—it's a set of spiritual truths and principles that guard our hearts and minds in Christ. From the shield of faith to the helmet of salvation, each piece serves a unique purpose in keeping us grounded in God's truth and protected from the enemy's schemes. When we fully "put on" this armor, we are aligning ourselves with God's power, resisting temptation, and standing firm in His promises.

This week, we'll dive deeper into the final elements of the armor of God and discover practical ways to incorporate them into our daily lives. Reflect on how you can make each piece an active part of your spiritual walk. Are you relying on the shield of faith when doubts arise? Are you using the sword of the Spirit, God's Word, to combat lies? Remember, God has provided this armor not only for protection but to equip you to live boldly and victoriously in His name.

1. **Focus:** Applying the remaining pieces of the armor of God.

2. **Key Scripture:** Ephesians 6:16-18

> *"6 in addition to all, taking up the shield of faith with which you will be able to extinguish all the flaming arrows of the evil one. 17 And take the helmet of salvation, and the sword of the Spirit, which is the word of God. 18 With all prayer and petition pray at all times in the Spirit, and with this in view, be on the alert with all perseverance and petition for all the saints,"*

3. **Discussion Questions:**

    1. How do the shield of faith, helmet of salvation, and sword of the Spirit protect and equip you for spiritual battle?

    ______________________________

    ______________________________

    ______________________________

    ______________________________

    ______________________________

    ______________________________

    ______________________________

    2. Why is prayer an essential part of spiritual warfare?

    ______________________________

    ______________________________

    ______________________________

    ______________________________

    ______________________________

    ______________________________

    ______________________________

4. **Action Step:** Study the final three pieces of the armor: the shield of faith, the helmet of salvation, and the sword of the Spirit. Reflect on how to actively use these pieces in daily spiritual warfare.

    1. The Shield of Faith:

    2. The Helmet of Salvation:

    3. The Sword of the Spirit:

5. **Man Up Challenge:** Pray the full armor of God over yourself each day this week, focusing on using your faith, salvation, and the Word of God as powerful tools in your spiritual battles.

**Week 35**: *Proverbs 1–16; John 13–14*

**Week 35- Accountability Questions for You and/ or Your Group: (End each week, holding each other accountable with these questions. Be honest, this is where we grow.)**

| | | Yes | No |
|---|---|---|---|
| 1. | Have you spent daily time in the Scriptures and in prayer? | | |
| 2. | Have you had any impure thoughts that would not glorify God? | | |
| 3. | Have you been completely above reproach in your financial dealings? | | |
| 4. | Have you spent quality relationship time with family and friends? | | |
| 5. | Have you done your 100% best in your job, school, home, etc.? | | |
| 6. | Have you told any half-truths or outright lies, putting yourself in a better light to those around you? | | |
| 7. | Have you shared the Gospel with an unbeliever this week? | | |
| 8. | Have you taken care of your body through daily physical exercise and proper eating/sleeping habits? | | |
| 9. | Have you allowed any person or circumstance to rob you of your joy? | | |
| 10. | Have you lied on any of your answers today? | | |

| Prayer Request | Name 5 People To Pray for this Week |
|---|---|
| • ______________________ | • ______________________ |
| • ______________________ | • ______________________ |
| • ______________________ | • ______________________ |
| • ______________________ | • ______________________ |
| • ______________________ | • ______________________ |
| • ______________________ | • ______________________ |
| • ______________________ | • ______________________ |

**Each week, we will give you men in the Bible who exemplified the main theme. Take time this week to study these men.**

**1. Abraham – Living by Faith (Shield of Faith)**

- Scripture: Romans 4:20-21
  "Yet, with respect to the promise of God, he did not waver in unbelief but grew strong in faith, giving glory to God, and being fully assured that what God had promised, He was also able to perform."

- Overview: Abraham's unwavering faith in God's promises exemplifies the shield of faith. Despite the impossibility of his circumstances—being promised a child in old age—Abraham trusted God completely. His faith protected him from doubt and discouragement, enabling him to stand firm and glorify God even when the fulfillment of the promise seemed distant.

**2. Paul – Confident in Salvation (Helmet of Salvation)**

- Scripture: 2 Timothy 4:7-8
  "I have fought the good fight, I have finished the course, I have kept the faith; in the future the crown of righteousness is reserved for me, which the Lord, the righteous Judge, will award to me on that day; and not only to me, but also to all who have loved His appearing."

- Overview: Paul exemplified the helmet of salvation by living with confidence in his eternal hope. His assurance of salvation allowed him to endure persecution, suffering, and hardship without wavering. Paul's focus on the crown of righteousness highlights his unshakable belief in God's promises and the ultimate victory of eternal life.

**3. Jesus – Speaking the Word of God (Sword of the Spirit)**

- Scripture: Matthew 4:4
  "But He answered and said, 'It is written: "Man shall not live on bread alone, but on every word that comes out of the mouth of God."'"

- Overview: When Jesus faced temptation in the wilderness, He wielded the sword of the Spirit—the Word of God. Each time Satan tempted Him, Jesus responded by quoting Scripture, countering the lies of the enemy with the truth of God's Word. Jesus' reliance on Scripture shows the power of God's Word in defending against spiritual attacks and standing firm in truth.

*"The armor of God is a daily reminder that we are in a battle, but we do not fight alone. Each piece equips us to stand firm in truth, faith, and righteousness, relying on God's strength to overcome every challenge."— John Piper*

# STANDING FIRM IN THE BATTLE

## WEEK 36: STANDING FIRM IN THE BATTLE

Life as a follower of Christ is a journey of faith, often met with spiritual opposition that challenges our beliefs and commitment. Yet, in the face of these battles, God calls us to stand firm, grounded in His strength and equipped with His armor. In Ephesians 6:13 (NASB), Paul instructs believers to *"take up the full armor of God, so that you will be able to resist in the evil day, and having done everything, to stand firm."* Standing firm is not about passively enduring; it's about actively leaning on God's truth and preparing ourselves to withstand and overcome the enemy's attacks.

To stand firm, we must be alert and prepared, rooted in God's Word and empowered by prayer. This unwavering stance requires faith, resilience, and a commitment to trust God even in the most difficult moments. It means choosing hope over despair, strength over weakness, and courage over fear. Through God's provision, we are equipped to face spiritual battles with confidence, knowing that He is our defender.

This week, we'll delve into the meaning of standing firm in spiritual warfare, exploring how to rely on God's strength and remain steadfast in faith. Take time to reflect on the areas of your life where you need to strengthen your defenses. Are you fully equipped with the armor of God? Are you prepared to face challenges with faith and resolve? Remember, God stands with you, empowering you to hold your ground in every battle.

- **Focus:** Engaging in spiritual battles with perseverance and confidence in God's strength.
- **Key Scriptures:** Ephesians 6:10-18, 2 Corinthians 10:3-5
- **Discussion Questions:**

1. How does wearing the full armor of God help you stand firm in the face of spiritual attacks?

________________________________________

________________________________________

________________________________________

________________________________________

________________________________________

________________________________________

________________________________________

________________________________________

2. What steps can you take to persevere in spiritual warfare, trusting God's strength rather than your own?

________________________________________

________________________________________

________________________________________

________________________________________

________________________________________

________________________________________

________________________________________

________________________________________

________________________________________

________________________________________

- **Action Step:** Reflect on your journey through this study and evaluate how wearing the armor of God has strengthened you in spiritual warfare. Identify any areas where you need further growth or preparation.

______________________________________________

______________________________________________

______________________________________________

______________________________________________

______________________________________________

______________________________________________

- **Man Up Challenge:** Continue to pray the armor of God over yourself daily. Share your experiences of spiritual warfare and victory with another brother in Christ, encouraging each other to stand firm in the faith.

______________________________________________

______________________________________________

______________________________________________

______________________________________________

______________________________________________

______________________________________________

**Ongoing Application:**

- **Daily Discipline:** Continue to wear the full armor of God in your daily life, relying on His strength in spiritual battles. Pray on all occasions and remain alert to the enemy's schemes.
- **Accountability:** Partner with a fellow believer to support and pray for each other in the face of spiritual warfare. Hold each other accountable for staying equipped with the armor of God.

**Week 36 Bible Reading**: *Proverbs 17–31; Ecclesiastes 1–8; John 15–16*

## Using the 22 Questions for Accountability

John Wesley and his Holy Club were renowned for their dedication to spiritual growth and rigorous accountability. At the heart of their gatherings were 22 questions that challenged each member to examine their faith, actions, and intentions. These questions were designed to help men remain focused on their walk with Christ, to grow in holiness, and to hold each other accountable to living out the Gospel daily.

In a world full of distractions and temptations, it's easy to drift in our spiritual lives without even realizing it. The 22 questions serve as a powerful tool to bring us back into alignment with God's will and to cultivate a life of intentional faith. They cover areas such as integrity, personal holiness, and commitment to spiritual disciplines, calling us to examine our hearts deeply and honestly.

Using these questions for accountability, whether in a group setting or personal reflection, can strengthen your walk with Christ by fostering humility, transparency, and a commitment to spiritual growth. As we go through these questions, consider how they apply to your life and how you can use them to grow as a man of God. True accountability isn't just about pointing out faults; it's about walking alongside one another, encouraging one another, and pushing one another toward holiness.

In your final week for this session, we encourage you to reflect on these questions with a trusted brother in Christ. Reflect and review the past four weeks and check your **prayer request** and the people you are praying for. Did you see God move? Allow these questions to challenge you to greater faithfulness, as they have for countless men of faith through the centuries.

1. Am I consciously or unconsciously creating the impression that I am better than I really am? In other words, am I a hypocrite?
2. Am I honest in all my acts and words, or do I exaggerate?
3. Do I confidentially pass on to another what was told to me in confidence?
4. Can I be trusted?
5. Am I a slave to dress, friends, work, or habits?
6. Am I self-conscious, self-pitying, or self-justifying?
7. Did the Bible live in me today?

8. Do I give it time to speak to me everyday?
9. Am I enjoying prayer?
10. When did I last speak to someone else about my faith?
11. Do I pray about the money I spend?
12. Do I get to bed on time and get up on time?
13. Do I disobey God in anything?
14. Do I insist upon doing something about which my conscience is uneasy?
15. Am I defeated in any part of my life?
16. Am I jealous, impure, critical, irritable, touchy, or distrustful?
17. How do I spend my spare time?
18. Am I proud?
19. Do I thank God that I am not as other people, especially as the Pharisees who despised the publican?
20. Is there anyone whom I fear, dislike, disown, criticize, hold a resentment toward or disregard? If so, what am I doing about it?
21. Do I grumble or complain constantly?
22. Is Christ real to me?

*"Standing firm in the battle means trusting God's strength over your own. It's not about avoiding the fight but stepping into it with the confidence that God has already equipped you for victory."*— **Jody Burkeen**

# CHAPTER 10
# PERSEVERANCE THROUGH TRIALS

# FINDING JOY IN TRIALS

## WEEK 37: FINDING JOY IN TRIALS

Trials are an inevitable part of life, but they don't have to define us or defeat us. As believers, we're called to approach hardships differently—not with despair, but with faith and even joy. James 1:2-3 reminds us, *"Consider it all joy, my brothers and sisters, when you encounter various trials, knowing that the testing of your faith produces endurance."* Trials, though difficult, are opportunities for spiritual growth and a deeper reliance on God.

Finding joy in trials doesn't mean denying the pain or pretending everything is fine. Instead, it means trusting that God is at work, using even our struggles to shape us into the people He's called us to be. Joy comes from knowing that trials refine our faith, strengthen our character, and draw us closer to God. It's about shifting our focus from the problem to the purpose, from our weakness to His strength.

This week, we'll explore how to find joy in the midst of trials, focusing on God's promises and His ability to bring beauty out of brokenness. Reflect on your current challenges and ask yourself: Am I trusting God to work through my trials? How can I shift my perspective to see His hand at work? Remember, trials are temporary, but the joy and growth they produce are eternal when we place our hope in Christ.

- Focus: Understanding the purpose of trials and finding joy in them.
- Key Scripture: James 1:2-4

> *"Consider it pure joy, my brothers and sisters, whenever you face trials of many kinds, because you know that the testing of your faith produces perseverance. Let perseverance finish its work so that you may be mature and complete, not lacking anything."*

- Discussion Questions:

1. How can you find joy in the midst of trials?

_______________________________________________

_______________________________________________

_______________________________________________

_______________________________________________

_______________________________________________

_______________________________________________

_______________________________________________

2. What is the connection between trials and spiritual maturity?

_______________________________________________

_______________________________________________

_______________________________________________

_______________________________________________

_______________________________________________

_______________________________________________

_______________________________________________

_______________________________________________

- Action Step: Reflect on a current or past trial in your life. Write down how this experience has tested your faith and how it has the potential to develop perseverance.

- Man Up Challenge: Focusing on how God is using your current trials to strengthen your faith and produce perseverance.

**Week 37- Accountability Questions for You and/ or Your Group: (End each week, holding each other accountable with these questions. Be honest, this is where we grow.)**

| | | Yes | No |
|---|---|---|---|
| 1. | Have you spent daily time in the Scriptures and in prayer? | | |
| 2. | Have you had any impure thoughts that would not glorify God? | | |
| 3. | Have you been completely above reproach in your financial dealings? | | |
| 4. | Have you spent quality relationship time with family and friends? | | |
| 5. | Have you done your 100% best in your job, school, home, etc.? | | |
| 6. | Have you told any half-truths or outright lies, putting yourself in a better light to those around you? | | |
| 7. | Have you shared the Gospel with an unbeliever this week? | | |
| 8. | Have you taken care of your body through daily physical exercise and proper eating/sleeping habits? | | |
| 9. | Have you allowed any person or circumstance to rob you of your joy? | | |
| 10. | Have you lied on any of your answers today? | | |

**Prayer Request**

- ____________________
- ____________________
- ____________________
- ____________________
- ____________________
- ____________________
- ____________________

**Name 5 People To Pray for this Week**

- ____________________
- ____________________
- ____________________
- ____________________
- ____________________
- ____________________
- ____________________

**Each week, we will give you men in the Bible who exemplified the main theme. Take time this week to study these men.**

### 1. JOB - TRUSTING GOD AMID PROFOUND SUFFERING

- Scripture: Job 1:21

  *"He said, 'Naked I came from my mother's womb, and naked I shall return there. The Lord gave and the Lord has taken away. Blessed be the name of the Lord.'"*

- Overview: Despite losing his possessions, family, and health, Job chose to worship and praise God, demonstrating a heart of trust even in overwhelming trials. While he struggled with questions and grief, his faith in God's sovereignty remained steadfast, allowing him to find hope and endurance in his suffering.

### 2. PAUL - REJOICING IN PERSECUTION FOR THE GOSPEL

- Scripture: Philippians 4:12-13

  *"I know how to get along with little, and I also know how to live in prosperity; in any and every circumstance I have learned the secret of being filled and going hungry, both of having abundance and suffering need. I can do all things through Him who strengthens me."*

- Overview: Paul faced countless trials-imprisonment, beatings, shipwrecks, and rejection-yet he consistently wrote about rejoicing in the Lord. His letters, particularly Philippians, often emphasize joy in Christ, regardless of circumstances. Paul's focus on God's strength and the eternal purpose of his trials allowed him to endure with joy.

### 3. JOSEPH - REMAINING FAITHFUL THROUGH INJUSTICE

- Scripture: Genesis 50:20

  *"As for you, you meant evil against me, but God meant it for good in order to bring about this present result, to keep many people alive."*

- Overview: Joseph faced betrayal by his brothers, enslavement, and imprisonment, yet he remained faithful to God and eventually saw how his trials were part of a greater plan. His ability to trust God's purpose through years of suffering allowed him to look back on his trials with joy, knowing they led to God's providential outcome.

> *"Trials are not evidence of God's absence; they are opportunities for His presence to be revealed. Joy comes when we trust that God is using our pain to shape us into who He's called us to be."* — **Tim Keller**

# HOPE IN SUFFERING

## WEEK 38: HOPE IN SUFFERING

Suffering is an unavoidable part of life, but for believers, it's not without purpose or hope. The Bible reminds us that God is present in our pain, using even the hardest seasons to draw us closer to Him and shape our character. Romans 5:3-5 declares, *"And not only this, but we also celebrate in our tribulations, knowing that tribulation brings about perseverance; and perseverance, proven character; and proven character, hope. And hope does not disappoint, because the love of God has been poured out within our hearts through the Holy Spirit who was given to us."*

Hope in suffering doesn't mean denying the reality of pain. It means trusting in God's sovereignty and His promises, knowing that He is working all things for good, even when we can't see the outcome. This hope is rooted in the assurance that God is with us, that His plans for us are good, and that He will bring redemption through every trial. When we fix our eyes on Him, our suffering becomes an opportunity to grow in faith, perseverance, and trust.

This week, we'll explore what it means to hold onto hope in the midst of suffering, focusing on the ways God brings purpose and redemption through our trials. Reflect on your own struggles and ask yourself: Am I trusting God to work through my pain? How can I lean into His promises when I feel overwhelmed? Remember, our hope is not in the temporary things of this world, but in the eternal love and faithfulness of our Savior.

- Focus: Recognizing that trials produce hope through perseverance.
- Key Scripture: Romans 5:3-5

> *"Not only so, but we also glory in our sufferings, because we know that suffering produces perseverance; perseverance, character; and character, hope. And hope does not put us to shame, because God's love has been poured out into our hearts through the Holy Spirit, who has been given to us."*

- Discussion Questions:

1. How does suffering lead to perseverance, and how does perseverance build hope?

2. How can God's love sustain you in times of trial?

- Action Step: Identify the character traits God is building in you through your current trials. Reflect on how these traits are contributing to your spiritual growth and hope in Christ.

- Man Up Challenge: Continue journaling, specifically documenting how God is developing perseverance, character, and hope in your life through trials.

**Week 38- Accountability Questions for You and/ or Your Group: (End each week holding each other accountable with these questions. Be honest, this is where we grow.)**

| | | Yes | No |
|---|---|---|---|
| 1. | Have you spent daily time in the Scriptures and in prayer? | | |
| 2. | Have you had any impure thoughts that would not glorify God? | | |
| 3. | Have you been completely above reproach in your financial dealings? | | |
| 4. | Have you spent quality relationship time with family and friends? | | |
| 5. | Have you done your 100% best in your job, school, home, etc.? | | |
| 6. | Have you told any half-truths or outright lies, putting yourself in a better light to those around you? | | |
| 7. | Have you shared the Gospel with an unbeliever this week? | | |
| 8. | Have you taken care of your body through daily physical exercise and proper eating/sleeping habits? | | |
| 9. | Have you allowed any person or circumstance to rob you of your joy? | | |
| 10. | Have you lied on any of your answers today? | | |

**Prayer Request**

- ______________________________
- ______________________________
- ______________________________
- ______________________________
- ______________________________
- ______________________________
- ______________________________

**Name 5 People To Pray for this Week**

- ______________________________
- ______________________________
- ______________________________
- ______________________________
- ______________________________
- ______________________________
- ______________________________

**Each week, we will give you men in the Bible who exemplified the main theme. Take time this week to study these men.**

### 1. JOB – TRUSTING GOD THROUGH PROFOUND LOSS

- Scripture: Job 19:25-26
  "Yet as for me, I know that my Redeemer lives, and at the last He will take His stand on the earth. Even after my skin is destroyed, yet from my flesh I will see God."
- Overview: Job endured unimaginable suffering—losing his children, wealth, and health—yet he held onto hope in God's ultimate justice and redemption. Despite his questions and anguish, Job's declaration of faith in his Redeemer shows his unwavering hope that God would restore him and vindicate his trust.

### 2. JOSEPH – TRUSTING GOD'S PLAN AMID INJUSTICE

- Scripture: Genesis 50:20
  "As for you, you meant evil against me, but God meant it for good in order to bring about this present result, to keep many people alive."
- Overview: Betrayed by his brothers, sold into slavery, and wrongfully imprisoned, Joseph endured years of suffering without losing hope in God's plan. When God elevated him to a position of influence, Joseph recognized that his suffering had a greater purpose, bringing life and provision to many.

### 3. PAUL – REJOICING IN HOPE DURING PERSECUTION

- Scripture: 2 Corinthians 4:16-18
  "Therefore we do not lose heart, but though our outer person is decaying, yet our inner person is being renewed day by day. For our momentary, light affliction is producing for us an eternal weight of glory far beyond all comparison, while we look not at the things which are seen, but at the things which are not seen."
- Overview: Paul endured beatings, imprisonment, shipwrecks, and rejection, yet he continually expressed hope in God's eternal purposes. His focus on the glory of eternity allowed him to see his suffering as temporary and meaningful, giving him the strength to press on with joy and perseverance.

*"Hope in suffering is not about denying the pain; it's about trusting God's purpose. When we anchor our hearts in His promises, we can endure the trials, knowing He is working all things for His glory and our good."*

***— Jody Burkeen***

# TRUSTING GOD'S PLAN

## WEEK 39: TRUSTING GOD'S PLAN

Life often takes unexpected turns, and in those moments, it can be challenging to understand what God is doing. Trusting God's plan requires faith in His sovereignty and goodness, even when His ways don't make sense to us. Proverbs 3:5-6 (NASB) reminds us, *"Trust in the Lord with all your heart and do not lean on your own understanding. In all your ways acknowledge Him, and He will make your paths straight."* Trusting God means surrendering our own understanding and placing our confidence in His perfect wisdom and timing.

God's plan for our lives is always for our good and His glory, even when it includes seasons of waiting, hardship, or uncertainty. While we may not always see the full picture, we can rest in the assurance that He is in control and working all things together for a greater purpose. Trusting God's plan requires patience, humility, and a willingness to let go of our desire for control, allowing Him to lead us where He knows is best.

This week, we'll explore what it means to trust God's plan, even in the face of uncertainty or difficulty. Reflect on areas in your life where you may be struggling to surrender to His will. Are you leaning on your own understanding, or are you relying on God's promises? Remember, God's plan is always greater than anything we could imagine, and when we trust Him, He will guide us on the right path.

- **Focus:** Trusting God's sovereignty and purpose in the midst of trials.
- **Key Scripture:** Proverbs 3:5-6

> *"Trust in the Lord with all your heart and lean not on your own understanding; in all your ways submit to him, and he will make your paths straight."*

- **Discussion Questions:**

1. What does it mean to trust in God rather than your own understanding during trials?

2. How can submitting to God's plan bring peace in difficult circumstances?

- **Action Step:** Write out a prayer surrendering your trials to God and committing to trust His plan, even when you don't fully understand it.

- **Man Up Challenge:** Share your experiences of trusting God through trials with a close friend or accountability partner. Discuss how God has been faithful in leading you through challenging times.

**Week 39- Accountability Questions for You and/ or Your Group: (End each week holding each other accountable with these questions. Be honest, this is where we grow.)**

| | | Yes | No |
|---|---|---|---|
| 1. | Have you spent daily time in the Scriptures and in prayer? | | |
| 2. | Have you had any impure thoughts that would not glorify God? | | |
| 3. | Have you been completely above reproach in your financial dealings? | | |
| 4. | Have you spent quality relationship time with family and friends? | | |
| 5. | Have you done your 100% best in your job, school, home, etc.? | | |
| 6. | Have you told any half-truths or outright lies, putting yourself in a better light to those around you? | | |
| 7. | Have you shared the Gospel with an unbeliever this week? | | |
| 8. | Have you taken care of your body through daily physical exercise and proper eating/sleeping habits? | | |
| 9. | Have you allowed any person or circumstance to rob you of your joy? | | |
| 10. | Have you lied on any of your answers today? | | |

**Prayer Request**

- ____________________
- ____________________
- ____________________
- ____________________
- ____________________
- ____________________
- ____________________

**Name 5 People To Pray for this Week**

- ____________________
- ____________________
- ____________________
- ____________________
- ____________________
- ____________________
- ____________________

**Each week, we will give you men in the Bible who exemplified the main theme. Take time this week to study these men.**

### 1. ABRAHAM – TRUSTING GOD'S PROMISE DESPITE UNCERTAINTY

- Scripture: Genesis 12:1-2
  "Now the Lord said to Abram, 'Go from your country, and from your relatives and from your father's house, to the land which I will show you; and I will make you into a great nation, and I will bless you, and make your name great; and you shall be a blessing.'"

- Overview: Abraham trusted God's plan when he was called to leave his home and go to a land God promised to show him, even though he didn't know where he was going. Later, he demonstrated faith again when God promised him a son in his old age, trusting that God would fulfill His promise despite impossible circumstances.

### 2. JOSEPH – TRUSTING GOD THROUGH TRIALS AND INJUSTICE

- Scripture: Genesis 50:20
  "As for you, you meant evil against me, but God meant it for good in order to bring about this present result, to keep many people alive."

- Overview: Betrayed by his brothers, sold into slavery, and falsely imprisoned, Joseph faced years of hardship but continued to trust God's plan. When God elevated him to a position of authority in Egypt, Joseph saw how his suffering was part of a larger plan to save many lives during a famine.

### 3. PAUL – TRUSTING GOD'S PLAN THROUGH SUFFERING FOR THE GOSPEL

- Scripture: Acts 20:22-24
  "And now, behold, bound by the Spirit, I am on my way to Jerusalem, not knowing what will happen to me there, except that the Holy Spirit solemnly testifies to me in every city, saying that chains and afflictions await me. But I do not consider my life of any account as dear to myself, so that I may finish my course and the ministry which I received from the Lord Jesus."

- Overview: Paul trusted God's plan even when it meant enduring suffering, persecution, and imprisonment. He remained focused on spreading the Gospel, confident that God's purpose was greater than his personal comfort or safety. Paul's unwavering commitment shows his trust in God's ultimate plan for his life and ministry.

> *"God's plan is often different from ours, but it's always better. Trusting Him means believing that His wisdom, timing, and purpose are perfect—even when we don't understand."* — ***Charles Stanley***

# STRENGTHENING FAITH THROUGH TRIALS

## WEEK 40: STRENGTHENING FAITH THROUGH TRIALS

Trials are an inevitable part of life, but they are also opportunities for growth and transformation. While challenges can test our faith, they are also the very moments that refine and strengthen it. James 1:2-3 (NASB) encourages us with this perspective: *"Consider it all joy, my brothers and sisters, when you encounter various trials, knowing that the testing of your faith produces endurance."* Trials are not meaningless—they are tools God uses to shape our character, deepen our trust in Him, and build a stronger, more resilient faith.

Strengthening faith through trials means learning to rely on God's promises when circumstances seem overwhelming. It's about choosing to trust His goodness, even when life feels uncertain or painful. Just as muscles grow stronger through resistance, our faith grows stronger when we face adversity with a heart focused on God. These moments remind us of our dependence on Him and His faithfulness to sustain us.

This week, we'll explore how trials can deepen your faith and draw you closer to God. Reflect on the challenges you've faced or are currently experiencing. How is God using them to grow your faith and shape your character? Are you leaning into His strength or trying to endure on your own? Remember, trials are not the end of the story—they are the pathway to a deeper relationship with God and a faith that can withstand life's storms.

- **Focus:** Building unshakable faith through enduring trials.
- **Key Scriptures:** James 1:2-4, Romans 5:3-5
- **Discussion Questions:**

1. How has your faith been strengthened through trials?

2. In what ways has God revealed His faithfulness to you during difficult times?

- **Action Step:** Review your journal entries from the past three weeks. Reflect on how God has been faithful and how your faith has grown. Identify areas where you still need to trust God more fully.

_______________________________________________

_______________________________________________

_______________________________________________

_______________________________________________

_______________________________________________

_______________________________________________

_______________________________________________

- **Man Up Challenge:** Write a letter to yourself or a loved one summarizing how God has strengthened your faith through trials. Use this letter as a testimony to God's faithfulness and as an encouragement for future challenges.

_______________________________________________

_______________________________________________

_______________________________________________

_______________________________________________

_______________________________________________

_______________________________________________

_______________________________________________

**Ongoing Application:**

- Daily Discipline: Continue journaling regularly, focusing on God's faithfulness and the ways He is shaping your faith through trials. Use these reflections as reminders of His presence in difficult times.
- Accountability: Share your journey through trials with others in your church or men's group. Encourage one another to trust God and persevere in faith through life's challenges.

## Using the 22 Questions for Accountability

John Wesley and his Holy Club were renowned for their dedication to spiritual growth and rigorous accountability. At the heart of their gatherings were 22 questions that challenged each member to examine their faith, actions, and intentions. These questions were designed to help men remain focused on their walk with Christ, to grow in holiness, and to hold each other accountable to living out the Gospel daily.

In a world full of distractions and temptations, it's easy to drift in our spiritual lives without even realizing it. The 22 questions serve as a powerful tool to bring us back into alignment with God's will and to cultivate a life of intentional faith. They cover areas such as integrity, personal holiness, and commitment to spiritual disciplines, calling us to examine our hearts deeply and honestly.

Using these questions for accountability, whether in a group setting or personal reflection, can strengthen your walk with Christ by fostering humility, transparency, and a commitment to spiritual growth. As we go through these questions, consider how they apply to your life and how you can use them to grow as a man of God. True accountability isn't just about pointing out faults; it's about walking alongside one another, encouraging one another, and pushing one another toward holiness.

In your final week for this session, we encourage you to reflect on these questions with a trusted brother in Christ. Reflect and review the past four weeks and check your **prayer request** and the people you are praying for. Did you see God move? Allow these questions to challenge you to greater faithfulness, as they have for countless men of faith through the centuries.

1. Am I consciously or unconsciously creating the impression that I am better than I really am? In other words, am I a hypocrite?
2. Am I honest in all my acts and words, or do I exaggerate?
3. Do I confidentially pass on to another what was told to me in confidence?
4. Can I be trusted?
5. Am I a slave to dress, friends, work, or habits?
6. Am I self-conscious, self-pitying, or self-justifying?
7. Did the Bible live in me today?

8. Do I give it time to speak to me everyday?

9. Am I enjoying prayer?

10. When did I last speak to someone else about my faith?

11. Do I pray about the money I spend?

12. Do I get to bed on time and get up on time?

13. Do I disobey God in anything?

14. Do I insist upon doing something about which my conscience is uneasy?

15. Am I defeated in any part of my life?

16. Am I jealous, impure, critical, irritable, touchy, or distrustful?

17. How do I spend my spare time?

18. Am I proud?

19. Do I thank God that I am not as other people, especially as the Pharisees who despised the publican?

20. Is there anyone whom I fear, dislike, disown, criticize, hold a resentment toward or disregard? If so, what am I doing about it?

21. Do I grumble or complain constantly?

22. Is Christ real to me?

*"Trials aren't meant to break your faith; they're meant to build it. When you trust God in the storm, your faith becomes stronger, your character is refined, and your testimony shines brighter."— **Jody Burkeen***

# CHAPTER 11
# BIBLICAL BROTHERHOOD

# IRON SHARPENS IRON

## WEEK 41: IRON SHARPENS IRON

The journey of faith is not one we are meant to walk alone. God designed us to grow and thrive in community, where we encourage, challenge, and strengthen one another. Proverbs 27:17 illustrates this beautifully: *"As iron sharpens iron, so one person sharpens another."* This verse reminds us that relationships grounded in faith are a tool God uses to refine us, making us stronger and more effective in our walk with Him.

Iron sharpening iron requires honesty, accountability, and a willingness to both give and receive correction in love. It's about surrounding yourself with people who will challenge you to grow spiritually, call you to greater faithfulness, and walk alongside you in both victories and struggles. These relationships help us to stay focused on God, develop Christlike character, and live out our purpose with greater clarity and strength.

This week, we'll explore what it means to sharpen one another in faith, focusing on how godly relationships can deepen your spiritual maturity and strengthen your walk with Christ. Reflect on the people in your life who encourage and challenge you. Are you being intentional in those relationships? Are you helping others grow in their faith as well? Remember, God often uses others to shape us, and when we sharpen each other, we reflect His love and grace in powerful ways.

- Focus: The importance of sharpening one another through relationships.
- Key Scripture: Proverbs 27:17
  "As iron sharpens iron, so one person sharpens another."
- Discussion Questions:

  1. How have other men sharpened you in your walk with God?

  ______________________________
  ______________________________
  ______________________________
  ______________________________
  ______________________________
  ______________________________
  ______________________________
  ______________________________
  ______________________________

  2. Why is it essential to surround yourself with godly men who can challenge and encourage you?

  ______________________________
  ______________________________
  ______________________________
  ______________________________
  ______________________________
  ______________________________
  ______________________________
  ______________________________
  ______________________________

- Action Step: Identify one or two men in your life who have been a positive influence on your spiritual growth. Reach out to them and express your gratitude.

- Man Up Challenge: Begin meeting regularly with one of these men for prayer and accountability. Commit to being intentional about sharpening each other in your faith journey.

**Week 41- Accountability Questions for You and/ or Your Group: (End each week holding each other accountable with these questions. Be honest, this is where we grow.)**

| | | Yes | No |
|---|---|---|---|
| 1. | Have you spent daily time in the Scriptures and in prayer? | | |
| 2. | Have you had any impure thoughts that would not glorify God? | | |
| 3. | Have you been completely above reproach in your financial dealings? | | |
| 4. | Have you spent quality relationship time with family and friends? | | |
| 5. | Have you done your 100% best in your job, school, home, etc.? | | |
| 6. | Have you told any half-truths or outright lies, putting yourself in a better light to those around you? | | |
| 7. | Have you shared the Gospel with an unbeliever this week? | | |
| 8. | Have you taken care of your body through daily physical exercise and proper eating/sleeping habits? | | |
| 9. | Have you allowed any person or circumstance to rob you of your joy? | | |
| 10. | Have you lied on any of your answers today? | | |

**Prayer Request**

- ____________________
- ____________________
- ____________________
- ____________________
- ____________________
- ____________________
- ____________________

**Name 5 People To Pray for this Week**

- ____________________
- ____________________
- ____________________
- ____________________
- ____________________
- ____________________
- ____________________

**Each week, we will give you men in the Bible who exemplified the main theme. Take time this week to study these men.**

**1. Moses and Joshua – Mentoring and Equipping for Leadership**

- **Scripture:** Exodus 24:13
  *"So Moses got up along with Joshua his servant, and Moses went up to the mountain of God."*

- **Overview:** Moses mentored Joshua, preparing him to lead the Israelites after Moses' death. Through their relationship, Joshua learned faith, courage, and leadership. Moses challenged and sharpened Joshua, helping him grow into a strong and godly leader. Their bond reflects the power of mentorship in shaping the next generation of leaders.

**2. David and Jonathan – Encouraging Faith in Friendship**

- **Scripture:** 1 Samuel 23:16-17
  *"Then Jonathan, Saul's son, set out and went to David at Horesh, and encouraged him in God. He said to him, 'Do not be afraid, because the hand of my father Saul will not find you; and you will be king over Israel, and I will be second to you; and Saul my father knows that as well.'"*

- **Overview:** David and Jonathan's friendship was marked by mutual encouragement and loyalty. Jonathan supported David during difficult times, strengthening his faith and reminding him of God's promises. Their relationship demonstrates how godly friendships can sharpen and sustain us through trials and challenges.

**3. Paul and Timothy – Discipleship and Mutual Growth**

- **Scripture:** 2 Timothy 1:6-7
  *"For this reason I remind you to kindle afresh the gift of God which is in you through the laying on of my hands. For God has not given us a spirit of timidity, but of power and love and discipline."*

- **Overview:** Paul mentored Timothy, equipping him for ministry and encouraging him to be bold in his faith. Paul's guidance helped Timothy develop spiritual strength and confidence in his calling. At the same time, Timothy's growth and faithfulness were a source of joy and affirmation for Paul, reflecting the mutual sharpening that occurs in discipleship relationships.

> *"God uses the people around us to shape us, refine us, and draw us closer to Him. Iron sharpens iron, and together we grow stronger in faith and character."— **John Piper***

# ENCOURAGING ONE ANOTHER IN FAITH

## WEEK 42: ENCOURAGING ONE ANOTHER IN FAITH

The Christian walk was never meant to be a solo journey. God designed us to live in community, where we can uplift, support, and encourage one another in faith. Hebrews 10:24-25 reminds us, "Let's consider how to encourage one another in love and good deeds, not abandoning our own meeting together, as is the habit of some people, but encouraging one another; and all the more as you see the day drawing near." Encouragement is a vital part of our spiritual growth and perseverance, especially in times of doubt, struggle, or fatigue.

To encourage one another in faith means to remind each other of God's promises, to pray for one another, and to build each other up with words and actions that point back to Christ. When we encourage others, we strengthen their confidence in God's love and help them press on in their journey. At the same time, encouraging others often refreshes and strengthens our own faith.

This week, we'll explore the power of encouragement in building faith and unity within the body of Christ. Reflect on how you can be an encourager in your community. Are there people in your life who need to be reminded of God's faithfulness? How can you use your words and actions to inspire and uplift others? Remember, a simple act of encouragement can have a lasting impact, helping others to grow stronger in their faith and trust in God.

- Focus: Building relationships that encourage perseverance in faith.
- Key Scripture: Hebrews 10:24-25

> *"And let us consider how we may spur one another on toward love and good deeds, not giving up meeting together, as some are in the habit of doing, but encouraging one another—and all the more as you see the Day approaching."*

- Discussion Questions:

1. How can you encourage and spur other men on toward love and good deeds?

________________________________________

________________________________________

________________________________________

________________________________________

________________________________________

________________________________________

________________________________________

________________________________________

2. What are the benefits of meeting regularly with other godly men for fellowship?

________________________________________

________________________________________

________________________________________

________________________________________

________________________________________

________________________________________

________________________________________

________________________________________

- Action Step: If you are not already part of a men's group in your church, start one for fellowship and encouragement. Identify men in your church who might benefit from joining. List men you can ask to join you.

- Man Up Challenge: Commit to attending a men's group or Bible study consistently this month. Encourage the men in your group to continue meeting and holding each other accountable.

**Week 42- Accountability Questions for You and/ or Your Group: (End each week holding each other accountable with these questions. Be honest, this is where we grow.)**

| | | Yes | No |
|---|---|---|---|
| 1. | Have you spent daily time in the Scriptures and in prayer? | | |
| 2. | Have you had any impure thoughts that would not glorify God? | | |
| 3. | Have you been completely above reproach in your financial dealings? | | |
| 4. | Have you spent quality relationship time with family and friends? | | |
| 5. | Have you done your 100% best in your job, school, home, etc.? | | |
| 6. | Have you told any half-truths or outright lies, putting yourself in a better light to those around you? | | |
| 7. | Have you shared the Gospel with an unbeliever this week? | | |
| 8. | Have you taken care of your body through daily physical exercise and proper eating/sleeping habits? | | |
| 9. | Have you allowed any person or circumstance to rob you of your joy? | | |
| 10. | Have you lied on any of your answers today? | | |

**Prayer Request**

- ______________________
- ______________________
- ______________________
- ______________________
- ______________________
- ______________________
- ______________________

**Name 5 People To Pray for this Week**

- ______________________
- ______________________
- ______________________
- ______________________
- ______________________
- ______________________
- ______________________

**Each week, we will give you men in the Bible who exemplified the main theme. Take time this week to study these men.**

**1. Barnabas – The Son of Encouragement**

- **Scripture:** Acts 11:23-2
  *"Then when he arrived and witnessed the grace of God, he rejoiced and began to encourage them all with a resolute heart to remain true to the Lord; for he was a good man, and full of the Holy Spirit and faith. And considerable numbers were added to the Lord."*

- **Overview:** Barnabas, whose name means "son of encouragement," lived up to his name by consistently uplifting and supporting others in their faith. He encouraged new believers in Antioch to stay faithful to the Lord and played a key role in mentoring Paul during his early ministry. Barnabas's life exemplifies how encouragement can strengthen others and advance God's Kingdom.

**2. Jonathan – Strengthening David's Faith in Times of Trouble**

- **Scripture:** 1 Samuel 23:16-17
  *"Then Jonathan, Saul's son, set out and went to David at Horesh, and encouraged him in God. He said to him, 'Do not be afraid, because the hand of my father Saul will not find you; and you will be king over Israel, and I will be second to you.'"*

- **Overview:** Jonathan encouraged David during one of the most difficult periods of his life, strengthening his faith in God's plan and protection. Jonathan reminded David of God's promises, offering reassurance and support even at great personal risk. His unwavering loyalty and encouragement helped David persevere in his faith and calling.

**3. Paul – Encouraging Churches Through Letters and Ministry**

- **Scripture:** 1 Thessalonians 5:11
  *"Therefore, encourage one another and build one another up, just as you also are doing."*

- **Overview:** Paul frequently encouraged the early churches through his letters, reminding them of God's faithfulness and urging them to persevere in their faith. His words of encouragement often addressed specific struggles or doubts, offering practical advice and spiritual reassurance. Paul's example shows the importance of consistently building others up in their faith, even from a distance.

> *"Encouraging one another in faith isn't just a nice gesture—it's a responsibility. When we speak life, share truth, and remind others of God's promises, we strengthen their walk and our own."*— ***Jody Burkeen***

# BEARING ONE ANOTHER'S BURDENS

## WEEK 43: BEARING ONE ANOTHER'S BURDENS

Life's challenges can often feel overwhelming, but God never intended for us to carry our burdens alone. As believers, we are called to come alongside one another, offering support, encouragement, and prayer in times of need. Galatians 6:2 instructs us, *"Bear one another's burdens, and thereby fulfill the law of Christ."* This law is the law of love, modeled by Jesus Himself, who carried the ultimate burden of sin for us on the cross.

Bearing one another's burdens means stepping into someone else's struggle with compassion and humility. It's about sharing the weight of their pain, walking with them through their trials, and pointing them to the hope and strength found in Christ. This act of selfless love not only strengthens the one in need but also deepens our unity as the body of Christ.

This week, we'll explore what it means to bear one another's burdens and how this command reflects the heart of Christ. Reflect on those in your life who may need support or encouragement. Are you willing to step into their struggles and offer help? How can you be a source of hope and strength to someone else? Remember, when we carry one another's burdens, we fulfill Christ's command to love as He has loved us, creating a community where no one walks alone.

- Focus: Supporting each other through challenges and struggles.
- Key Scripture: Galatians 6:2

> *"Carry each other's burdens, and in this way you will fulfill the law of Christ."*

- Discussion Questions:

1. How can you be more intentional in helping other men carry their burdens?

_______________________________________________

_______________________________________________

_______________________________________________

_______________________________________________

_______________________________________________

_______________________________________________

_______________________________________________

_______________________________________________

2. Why is it important to have a group of godly men to turn to in times of difficulty?

_______________________________________________

_______________________________________________

_______________________________________________

_______________________________________________

_______________________________________________

_______________________________________________

_______________________________________________

_______________________________________________

_______________________________________________

- Action Step: Reach out to a man in your group or circle who is going through a difficult time. Offer to pray with him and provide practical support where possible. Name five men who you can pray for via call or text:

- Man Up Challenge: Commit to bearing the burdens of another brother this week, whether through prayer, encouragement, or practical help. Be proactive in checking in on his well-being.

**Week 43- Accountability Questions for You and/ or Your Group: (End each week holding each other accountable with these questions. Be honest, this is where we grow.)**

| | | Yes | No |
|---|---|---|---|
| 1. | Have you spent daily time in the Scriptures and in prayer? | | |
| 2. | Have you had any impure thoughts that would not glorify God? | | |
| 3. | Have you been completely above reproach in your financial dealings? | | |
| 4. | Have you spent quality relationship time with family and friends? | | |
| 5. | Have you done your 100% best in your job, school, home, etc.? | | |
| 6. | Have you told any half-truths or outright lies, putting yourself in a better light to those around you? | | |
| 7. | Have you shared the Gospel with an unbeliever this week? | | |
| 8. | Have you taken care of your body through daily physical exercise and proper eating/sleeping habits? | | |
| 9. | Have you allowed any person or circumstance to rob you of your joy? | | |
| 10. | Have you lied on any of your answers today? | | |

**Prayer Request**

- ____________________
- ____________________
- ____________________
- ____________________
- ____________________
- ____________________
- ____________________

**Name 5 People To Pray for this Week**

- ____________________
- ____________________
- ____________________
- ____________________
- ____________________
- ____________________
- ____________________

**Each week, we will give you men in the Bible who exemplified the main theme. Take time this week to study these men.**

### 1. MOSES – LEADING AND INTERCEDING FOR THE ISRAELITES

- Scripture: Exodus 17:11-12
  "So it came about, when Moses raised his hand, that Israel prevailed; but when he let his hand down, Amalek prevailed. And Moses' hands were heavy. So they took a stone and put it under him, and he sat on it; and Aaron and Hur supported his hands, one on one side and one on the other. So his hands were steady until the sun set."

- Overview: Moses carried the burden of leading the Israelites through the wilderness, often interceding for them and enduring their complaints. In moments of weakness, such as during the battle with Amalek, Aaron and Hur came alongside him to help bear the weight of his responsibility, enabling him to lead effectively. This illustrates the importance of sharing burdens for the sake of God's mission.

### 2. JONATHAN – PROTECTING AND ENCOURAGING DAVID

- Scripture: 1 Samuel 20:16-17
  "So Jonathan made a covenant with the house of David, saying, 'May the Lord demand it from the hands of David's enemies.' And Jonathan made David vow again because of his love for him, because he loved him as he loved his own life."

- Overview: Jonathan bore David's burdens by protecting him from King Saul's wrath and encouraging him to trust in God's plan. Jonathan risked his own position and safety to ensure David's well-being, showing a sacrificial love and commitment that strengthened David during his trials.

### 3. PAUL – CARRYING THE CONCERNS OF THE EARLY CHURCHES

- Scripture: 2 Corinthians 11:28-29
  "Apart from such external things, there is the daily pressure on me of concern for all the churches. Who is weak without my being weak? Who is led into sin without my intense concern?"

- Overview: Paul bore the spiritual and emotional burdens of the early churches, consistently interceding for them in prayer, writing letters of encouragement, and addressing their struggles. His deep concern for their spiritual growth and well-being reflects a heart willing to carry the weight of others' faith journeys.

> *"Encouraging one another in faith isn't just a nice gesture—it's a responsibility. When we speak life, share truth, and remind others of God's promises, we strengthen their walk and our own."*— ***Jody Burkeen***

# STRENGTHENING BROTHERHOOD IN CHRIST

## WEEK 44: STRENGTHENING BROTHERHOOD IN CHRIST

The Christian life is not meant to be lived in isolation. God designed us for community, and one of the most powerful relationships we can cultivate is the bond of brotherhood in Christ. Proverbs 27:17 (NASB) reminds us, *"As iron sharpens iron, so one person sharpens another."* Brotherhood in Christ goes beyond friendship—it is a deep, spiritual connection rooted in shared faith, mutual encouragement, and accountability. Together, brothers in Christ are stronger, better equipped to face life's challenges, and more effective in living out God's mission.

Strengthening brotherhood involves building relationships where trust, love, and honesty flourish. It means walking alongside one another through trials, celebrating victories, and holding each other accountable in faith. These relationships sharpen us spiritually, challenge us to grow, and remind us that we are not alone in our journey. In a world that often promotes self-reliance, brotherhood in Christ is a gift that provides support, unity, and a reflection of God's love.

This week, we'll explore how to strengthen the bond of brotherhood in Christ and why it is essential for spiritual growth. Reflect on the men in your life who support and challenge you in your faith. Are you investing in these relationships? How can you deepen your connection and become a better brother in Christ to others? Remember, a strong brotherhood glorifies God, builds His Kingdom, and reminds us of the strength we have when we walk together in faith.

- Focus: Growing deeper relationships with godly men that last a lifetime.
- Key Scriptures: Proverbs 27:17, Hebrews 10:24-25
- Discussion Questions:

3. How have your relationships with other men deepened your relationship with Christ?

4. What steps can you take to ensure that you maintain strong, accountable relationships with godly men in the future?

- Action Step: Reflect on how your relationship with your accountability group or men's group has grown. Make a plan to stay connected, even when life gets busy or difficult.

_______________________________________________

_______________________________________________

_______________________________________________

_______________________________________________

_______________________________________________

_______________________________________________

_______________________________________________

- Man Up Challenge: Solidify your commitment to regularly meeting with your men's group by creating a plan for ongoing fellowship. Share your commitment with the group and encourage each other to continue pursuing Christ together.

_______________________________________________

_______________________________________________

_______________________________________________

_______________________________________________

_______________________________________________

_______________________________________________

_______________________________________________

**Ongoing Application:**

- Daily Discipline: Continue building strong relationships with godly men, prioritizing fellowship, prayer, and accountability. Make time to meet regularly with your men's group.
- Accountability: Stay committed to your men's group or accountability partners. Regularly check in with each other, pray together, and provide encouragement and support.

## Using the 22 Questions for Accountability

John Wesley and his Holy Club were renowned for their dedication to spiritual growth and rigorous accountability. At the heart of their gatherings were 22 questions that challenged each member to examine their faith, actions, and intentions. These questions were designed to help men remain focused on their walk with Christ, to grow in holiness, and to hold each other accountable to living out the Gospel daily.

In a world full of distractions and temptations, it's easy to drift in our spiritual lives without even realizing it. The 22 questions serve as a powerful tool to bring us back into alignment with God's will and to cultivate a life of intentional faith. They cover areas such as integrity, personal holiness, and commitment to spiritual disciplines, calling us to examine our hearts deeply and honestly.

Using these questions for accountability, whether in a group setting or personal reflection, can strengthen your walk with Christ by fostering humility, transparency, and a commitment to spiritual growth. As we go through these questions, consider how they apply to your life and how you can use them to grow as a man of God. True accountability isn't just about pointing out faults; it's about walking alongside one another, encouraging one another, and pushing one another toward holiness.

In your final week for this session, we encourage you to reflect on these questions with a trusted brother in Christ. Reflect and review the past four weeks and check your **prayer request** and the people you are praying for. Did you see God move? Allow these questions to challenge you to greater faithfulness, as they have for countless men of faith through the centuries.

1. Am I consciously or unconsciously creating the impression that I am better than I really am? In other words, am I a hypocrite?
2. Am I honest in all my acts and words, or do I exaggerate?
3. Do I confidentially pass on to another what was told to me in confidence?
4. Can I be trusted?
5. Am I a slave to dress, friends, work, or habits?
6. Am I self-conscious, self-pitying, or self-justifying?
7. Did the Bible live in me today?

8. Do I give it time to speak to me everyday?
9. Am I enjoying prayer?
10. When did I last speak to someone else about my faith?
11. Do I pray about the money I spend?
12. Do I get to bed on time and get up on time?
13. Do I disobey God in anything?
14. Do I insist upon doing something about which my conscience is uneasy?
15. Am I defeated in any part of my life?
16. Am I jealous, impure, critical, irritable, touchy, or distrustful?
17. How do I spend my spare time?
18. Am I proud?
19. Do I thank God that I am not as other people, especially as the Pharisees who despised the publican?
20. Is there anyone whom I fear, dislike, disown, criticize, hold a resentment toward or disregard? If so, what am I doing about it?
21. Do I grumble or complain constantly?
22. Is Christ real to me?

*"True brotherhood in Christ isn't just about friendship; it's about accountability, encouragement, and a shared commitment to pursue God's purpose together. When we stand united in faith, we reflect the heart of Christ."*— ***John MacArthur***

# CHAPTER 12
# LEGACY OF FAITH

# THE CALL TO TEACH FUTURE GENERATIONS

## WEEK 45: THE CALL TO TEACH FUTURE GENERATIONS

The responsibility to teach future generations is one of the most vital and rewarding calls in the Christian life. Passing on the knowledge of God's Word, His promises, and His faithfulness ensures that the next generation grows up with a strong foundation of faith. Psalm 78:4 declares, *"We will not conceal them from their children, but we will tell the generation to come the praises of the Lord, and His power and His wondrous works that He has done."* This calling is not limited to parents; it extends to all believers who have the opportunity to invest in the lives of the next generation.

Teaching future generations requires intentionality, patience, and a commitment to living as an example of Christ's love. It's about more than just words—it's about demonstrating a life of faith, showing what it means to trust and follow God in everyday life. By planting seeds of truth and nurturing them with love and prayer, we equip the next generation to know God, stand firm in their faith, and share His message with others.

This week, we'll explore how to embrace the call to teach future generations, focusing on practical ways to invest in their spiritual growth. Reflect on the younger people in your life who need guidance and encouragement. Are you making the effort to share your faith with them? How can you model a life that inspires them to follow Christ? Remember, teaching the next generation is more than a duty—it's an opportunity to leave a lasting legacy of faith.

- Focus: Understanding the importance of teaching your children and others about God's commands.
- Key Scripture: Deuteronomy 6:6-9

> *"These commandments that I give you today are to be on your hearts. Impress them on your children. Talk about them when you sit at home and when you walk along the road, when you lie down and when you get up. Tie them as symbols on your hands and bind them on your foreheads. Write them on the doorframes of your houses and on your gates."*

- Discussion Questions:

1. What does it mean to impress God's commandments on your children and loved ones?

______________________________________________

______________________________________________

______________________________________________

______________________________________________

______________________________________________

______________________________________________

2. How can you make conversations about God a regular part of your daily life?

______________________________________________

______________________________________________

______________________________________________

______________________________________________

______________________________________________

______________________________________________

______________________________________________

- Action Step: Begin making a conscious effort to talk about God's commands and the principles of faith in everyday conversations with your family. (Link for a family devotion)

- Man Up Challenge: This week, start a spiritual conversation with your children, loved ones, or a younger believer. Share a specific way that God has been faithful in your life.

**Week 45- Accountability Questions for You and/ or Your Group: (End each week holding each other accountable with these questions. Be honest, this is where we grow.)**

| | | Yes | No |
|---|---|---|---|
| 1. | Have you spent daily time in the Scriptures and in prayer? | | |
| 2. | Have you had any impure thoughts that would not glorify God? | | |
| 3. | Have you been completely above reproach in your financial dealings? | | |
| 4. | Have you spent quality relationship time with family and friends? | | |
| 5. | Have you done your 100% best in your job, school, home, etc.? | | |
| 6. | Have you told any half-truths or outright lies, putting yourself in a better light to those around you? | | |
| 7. | Have you shared the Gospel with an unbeliever this week? | | |
| 8. | Have you taken care of your body through daily physical exercise and proper eating/sleeping habits? | | |
| 9. | Have you allowed any person or circumstance to rob you of your joy? | | |
| 10. | Have you lied on any of your answers today? | | |

| **Prayer Request** | **Name 5 People To Pray for this Week** |
|---|---|
| • ____________________ | • ____________________ |
| • ____________________ | • ____________________ |
| • ____________________ | • ____________________ |
| • ____________________ | • ____________________ |
| • ____________________ | • ____________________ |
| • ____________________ | • ____________________ |
| • ____________________ | • ____________________ |

**Each week, we will give you men in the Bible who exemplified the main theme. Take time this week to study these men.**

## 1. MOSES – TEACHING GOD'S LAW TO THE ISRAELITES

- Scripture: Deuteronomy 6:6-7
  "These words, which I am commanding you today, shall be on your heart. And you shall repeat them diligently to your sons and speak of them when you sit in your house, when you walk on the road, when you lie down, and when you get up."

- Overview: Moses emphasized the importance of teaching God's commands to the next generation so that they would remember and follow His ways. He instructed the Israelites to make God's Word central in their daily lives, ensuring that future generations would live faithfully in obedience to Him.

## 2. ASAPH – DECLARING GOD'S WORKS THROUGH PSALM 78

- Scripture: Psalm 78:4-7
  "We will not conceal them from their children, but we will tell the generation to come the praises of the Lord, and His power and His wondrous works that He has done... so that they may put their confidence in God and not forget the works of God, but comply with His commandments."

- Overview: Asaph, a leader of worship and writer of Psalms, highlighted the importance of recounting God's mighty deeds to future generations. His psalms served as a tool to remind children and descendants of God's faithfulness, encouraging them to trust in Him and live obediently.

## 3. PAUL – MENTORING TIMOTHY AND EQUIPPING HIM TO TEACH OTHERS

- Scripture: 2 Timothy 2:2
  "The things which you have heard from me in the presence of many witnesses, entrust these to faithful people who will be able to teach others also."

- Overview: Paul took the time to mentor Timothy, equipping him with sound doctrine and encouraging him to pass on what he had learned to others. Paul's discipleship ensured that the Gospel message would continue through generations of faithful teachers and leaders.

*"Teaching the next generation isn't just a responsibility—it's a legacy. When we pour God's truth into their lives, we equip them to stand firm in their faith and impact the world for His glory."* — ***Jody Burkeen***

# TELLING THE NEXT GENERATION

## WEEK 46: TELLING THE NEXT GENERATION

Passing down the truths of God's Word and His faithfulness is one of the greatest responsibilities and privileges we have as believers. The Bible commands us to share the stories of God's goodness, power, and love with the next generation so they, too, can walk in faith and obedience. Psalm 78:4 (NASB) declares, *"We will not conceal them from their children, but we will tell the generation to come the praises of the Lord, and His power and His wondrous works that He has done."* By sharing our testimonies and teaching biblical truth, we equip the next generation to trust in God and live for His purposes.

Telling the next generation involves more than just words; it's about living a life that reflects God's grace and truth, showing them what it means to walk faithfully with Him. When we share the lessons we've learned through God's faithfulness, we encourage and inspire the next generation to rely on Him in their own lives. It's about creating a ripple effect of faith that continues beyond our own lifetime.

This week, we'll explore the importance of telling the next generation about God's works and how we can do so with intentionality and love. Reflect on your own faith story—what lessons, experiences, or truths has God taught you that you can share? Are you actively investing in the spiritual growth of the next generation? Remember, the impact of your words and example can shape a legacy of faith that endures for generations.

- Focus: Passing on the stories of God's faithfulness to future generations.
- Key Scripture: Psalm 78:4-7

> *"We will not hide them from their descendants; we will tell the next generation the praiseworthy deeds of the Lord, his power, and the wonders he has done. He decreed statutes for Jacob and established the law in Israel, which he commanded our ancestors to teach their children, so the next generation would know them, even the children yet to be born, and they in turn would tell their children. Then they would put their trust in God and would not forget his deeds but would keep his commands."*

- Discussion Questions:

1. Why is it important to tell the next generation about God's faithfulness?

______________________________________________

______________________________________________

______________________________________________

______________________________________________

______________________________________________

______________________________________________

2. How can sharing stories of God's deeds help build trust in Him?

______________________________________________

______________________________________________

______________________________________________

______________________________________________

______________________________________________

______________________________________________

______________________________________________

- Action Step: Reflect on the major events in your life where God has been faithful. Write down these stories and be prepared to share them with your children or those you mentor.

- Man Up Challenge: Share one of these stories with someone in your family or your circle of influence. Encourage them to trust in God by learning from your experiences.

**Week 46- Accountability Questions for You and/ or Your Group: (End each week holding each other accountable with these questions. Be honest, this is where we grow.)**

| | | Yes | No |
|---|---|---|---|
| 1. | Have you spent daily time in the Scriptures and in prayer? | | |
| 2. | Have you had any impure thoughts that would not glorify God? | | |
| 3. | Have you been completely above reproach in your financial dealings? | | |
| 4. | Have you spent quality relationship time with family and friends? | | |
| 5. | Have you done your 100% best in your job, school, home, etc.? | | |
| 6. | Have you told any half-truths or outright lies, putting yourself in a better light to those around you? | | |
| 7. | Have you shared the Gospel with an unbeliever this week? | | |
| 8. | Have you taken care of your body through daily physical exercise and proper eating/sleeping habits? | | |
| 9. | Have you allowed any person or circumstance to rob you of your joy? | | |
| 10. | Have you lied on any of your answers today? | | |

**Prayer Request**

- ____________________
- ____________________
- ____________________
- ____________________
- ____________________
- ____________________
- ____________________

**Name 5 People To Pray for this Week**

- ____________________
- ____________________
- ____________________
- ____________________
- ____________________
- ____________________
- ____________________

**Each week, we will give you men in the Bible who exemplified the main theme. Take time this week to study these men.**

### 1. MOSES – TEACHING THE COMMANDMENTS TO FUTURE GENERATIONS

- Scripture: Deuteronomy 6:6-7
  "These words, which I am commanding you today, shall be on your heart. And you shall repeat them diligently to your sons and speak of them when you sit in your house, when you walk on the road, when you lie down, and when you get up."

- Overview: Moses commanded the Israelites to diligently teach God's laws to their children so that future generations would know and follow Him. He emphasized integrating God's Word into daily life, ensuring it was passed down as the foundation of faith and obedience.

### 2. JOSHUA – REMINDING ISRAEL OF GOD'S FAITHFULNESS

- Scripture: Joshua 24:15
  "But as for me and my house, we will serve the Lord."

- Overview: At the end of his life, Joshua gathered the Israelites to remind them of God's faithfulness and challenge them to commit their households to serve the Lord. He recounted how God delivered them from Egypt and provided for them in the Promised Land, ensuring the next generation remembered God's works.

### 3. DAVID – PROCLAIMING GOD'S GOODNESS TO FUTURE GENERATIONS

- Scripture: Psalm 145:4 (NASB)
  "One generation will praise Your works to another, and will declare Your mighty acts."

- Overview: David frequently wrote about the importance of telling future generations about God's mighty acts and faithfulness. Through his psalms, he created a legacy of worship and teaching that pointed others to the greatness of God, inspiring future generations to trust and follow Him.

*"We are one generation away from losing the Gospel. It is our sacred duty to tell the next generation of God's faithfulness, His works, and His truth so they may know Him and make Him known."* **— David Platt**

# MODELING A LIFE OF FAITH

## WEEK 47: MODELING A LIFE OF FAITH

Faith is not just something we talk about—it's something we live. The most powerful way to influence others for Christ, especially those closest to us, is by modeling a life of faith. When our actions align with our beliefs, we demonstrate what it means to truly walk with God. Matthew 5:16 (NASB) reminds us, *"Your light must shine before people in such a way that they may see your good works, and glorify your Father who is in heaven."* Living out our faith with integrity, consistency, and love serves as a testimony that points others to God.

Modeling a life of faith requires authenticity, humility, and reliance on God. It's not about perfection, but about demonstrating a genuine relationship with Him through our everyday actions, words, and decisions. When others see us trusting God in trials, loving sacrificially, and standing firm in our convictions, it inspires them to seek the same relationship with Christ.

This week, we'll explore the importance of modeling faith in your home, workplace, and community. Reflect on your life—does it reflect Christ to those around you? Are there areas where you can grow in demonstrating your faith more consistently? Remember, people are watching, and your life might be the example that leads someone else to a deeper faith in God.

- Focus: Living in a way that exemplifies faith in everyday life.
- Key Scripture: 1 Corinthians 11:1

> *"Follow my example, as I follow the example of Christ."*

- Discussion Questions:

1. What does it mean to be an example of faith that others can follow?

2. In what areas of your life do you need to become a better role model of faith?

- Action Step: Reflect on the ways your actions, words, and attitudes either reflect or contradict your faith. Make a plan to consistently model faith in your home and community.

- Man Up Challenge: This week, ask a trusted friend or family member to give you feedback on how well your life models faith. Use their input to make any necessary adjustments in your walk with Christ.

**Week 45- Accountability Questions for You and/ or Your Group: (End each week holding each other accountable with these questions. Be honest, this is where we grow.)**

| | | Yes | No |
|---|---|---|---|
| 1. | Have you spent daily time in the Scriptures and in prayer? | | |
| 2. | Have you had any impure thoughts that would not glorify God? | | |
| 3. | Have you been completely above reproach in your financial dealings? | | |
| 4. | Have you spent quality relationship time with family and friends? | | |
| 5. | Have you done your 100% best in your job, school, home, etc.? | | |
| 6. | Have you told any half-truths or outright lies, putting yourself in a better light to those around you? | | |
| 7. | Have you shared the Gospel with an unbeliever this week? | | |
| 8. | Have you taken care of your body through daily physical exercise and proper eating/sleeping habits? | | |
| 9. | Have you allowed any person or circumstance to rob you of your joy? | | |
| 10. | Have you lied on any of your answers today? | | |

**Prayer Request**

- ____________________
- ____________________
- ____________________
- ____________________
- ____________________
- ____________________
- ____________________

**Name 5 People To Pray for this Week**

- ____________________
- ____________________
- ____________________
- ____________________
- ____________________
- ____________________
- ____________________

**Each week, we will give you men in the Bible who exemplified the main theme. Take time this week to study these men.**

### 1. ENOCH – WALKING FAITHFULLY WITH GOD

- Scripture: Genesis 5:24
  "Enoch walked with God; and he was not, for God took him."

- Overview: Enoch's life was characterized by an unwavering walk with God. Though the details of his life are limited in Scripture, his faith and consistent relationship with God were so profound that he was taken to heaven without experiencing death. His example demonstrates the power of faithfully modeling a life devoted to God.

### 2. DANIEL – FAITHFUL IN EVERY CIRCUMSTANCE

- Scripture: Daniel 6:10
  "Now when Daniel learned that the document was signed, he entered his house (and in his roof chamber he had windows open toward Jerusalem); and he continued kneeling on his knees three times a day, praying and offering praise before his God, just as he had been doing previously."

- Overview: Daniel modeled unwavering faith in God, even under pressure to conform to worldly standards. His consistency in prayer and obedience, despite the threat of persecution, demonstrated to those around him what it meant to trust and follow God wholeheartedly. His faith influenced kings and nations.

- Key Reflection: How does Daniel's courage and consistency in faith encourage us to live boldly for God, no matter the circumstances?

### 3. PAUL – A LIFE TRANSFORMED BY FAITH

- Scripture: 1 Corinthians 11:1
  "Be imitators of me, just as I also am of Christ."

- Overview: Paul's life after his conversion exemplifies a complete transformation through faith. He devoted himself to spreading the Gospel, enduring persecution, and mentoring others in their walk with Christ. Paul's willingness to sacrifice everything for the sake of the Gospel serves as a powerful model of faith in action.

*"Modeling a life of faith isn't about perfection; it's about authenticity. When we live out our faith daily—trusting God, repenting when we fall, and loving others well—we show the world what it truly means to follow Christ."* — **Jody Burkeen**

# MENTORING THE NEXT GENERATION

## WEEK 48: MENTORING THE NEXT GENERATION

Mentoring the next generation is one of the most significant investments we can make for the Kingdom of God. As believers, we are called to guide, encourage, and equip younger generations to grow in their faith and live out their God-given purpose. In 2 Timothy 2:2, Paul writes, *"The things which you have heard from me in the presence of many witnesses, entrust these to faithful people who will be able to teach others also."* Mentoring is about passing on biblical wisdom, life experience, and spiritual truth to those who will carry the torch of faith forward.

Mentorship is more than teaching—it's walking alongside someone, modeling a Christ-centered life, and helping them navigate challenges with grace and truth. It requires time, patience, and a willingness to be vulnerable about your own struggles and victories. When we mentor others, we not only help them grow, but we also deepen our own faith as we see God at work in their lives.

This week, we'll explore the biblical principles of mentoring and the impact it can have on the next generation. Reflect on who God might be calling you to mentor. Are you intentional about pouring into their spiritual growth? Are you living a life that points them to Christ? Remember, mentoring is not just a duty; it's a privilege to help shape the lives of those who will carry God's truth to the future.

- Focus: Investing in younger believers and passing on your faith to them.
- Key Scriptures: Deuteronomy 6:6-9, Psalm 78:4-7
- Discussion Questions:

1. What is the impact of mentoring a younger person in the faith?

2. How can you be more intentional about discipling someone younger in their spiritual walk?

- Action Step: Write a letter to your children or a younger man you are mentoring, sharing your faith journey, how God has worked in your life, and the lessons you want to pass on to them.

_______________________________________________

_______________________________________________

_______________________________________________

_______________________________________________

_______________________________________________

_______________________________________________

_______________________________________________

- Man Up Challenge: Commit to mentoring a younger man in the faith. Set up a time to meet regularly, pray together, and share biblical truths that will help him grow in his relationship with God.

_______________________________________________

_______________________________________________

_______________________________________________

_______________________________________________

_______________________________________________

_______________________________________________

_______________________________________________

## Ongoing Application:

- Daily Discipline: Continue investing in future generations by sharing stories of God's faithfulness and living as an example of faith. Make mentoring and discipleship a consistent part of your life.
- Accountability: Stay accountable to a fellow believer as you mentor others and seek to leave a spiritual legacy. Encourage each other in your role as spiritual leaders for the next generation.

### Week 48 Using the 22 Questions for Accountability

John Wesley and his Holy Club were renowned for their dedication to spiritual growth and rigorous accountability. At the heart of their gatherings were 22 questions that challenged each member to examine their faith, actions, and intentions. These questions were designed to help men remain focused on their walk with Christ, to grow in holiness, and to hold each other accountable to living out the Gospel daily.

In a world full of distractions and temptations, it's easy to drift in our spiritual lives without even realizing it. The 22 questions serve as a powerful tool to bring us back into alignment with God's will and to cultivate a life of intentional faith. They cover areas such as integrity, personal holiness, and commitment to spiritual disciplines, calling us to examine our hearts deeply and honestly.

Using these questions for accountability, whether in a group setting or personal reflection, can strengthen your walk with Christ by fostering humility, transparency, and a commitment to spiritual growth. As we go through these questions, consider how they apply to your life and how you can use them to grow as a man of God. True accountability isn't just about pointing out faults; it's about walking alongside one another, encouraging one another, and pushing one another toward holiness.

In your final week for this session, we encourage you to reflect on these questions with a trusted brother in Christ. Reflect and review the past four weeks and check your **prayer request** and the people you are praying for. Did you see God move? Allow these questions to challenge you to greater faithfulness, as they have for countless men of faith through the centuries.

1. Am I consciously or unconsciously creating the impression that I am better than I really am? In other words, am I a hypocrite?
2. Am I honest in all my acts and words, or do I exaggerate?
3. Do I confidentially pass on to another what was told to me in confidence?
4. Can I be trusted?
5. Am I a slave to dress, friends, work, or habits?
6. Am I self-conscious, self-pitying, or self-justifying?
7. Did the Bible live in me today?

8. Do I give it time to speak to me everyday?
9. Am I enjoying prayer?
10. When did I last speak to someone else about my faith?
11. Do I pray about the money I spend?
12. Do I get to bed on time and get up on time?
13. Do I disobey God in anything?
14. Do I insist upon doing something about which my conscience is uneasy?
15. Am I defeated in any part of my life?
16. Am I jealous, impure, critical, irritable, touchy, or distrustful?
17. How do I spend my spare time?
18. Am I proud?
19. Do I thank God that I am not as other people, especially as the Pharisees who despised the publican?
20. Is there anyone whom I fear, dislike, disown, criticize, hold a resentment toward or disregard? If so, what am I doing about it?
21. Do I grumble or complain constantly?
22. Is Christ real to me?

> *"Mentoring is more than teaching; it's pouring your life into others, so they can see Christ in you and be inspired to follow Him more closely."*— ***Billy Graham***

# CONCLUSION

As you complete this 12-month journey of discipleship, take a moment to reflect on the transformation God has been working in your life. From deepening your understanding of biblical manhood to overcoming temptation, from building spiritual disciplines to leading in your home, you have taken deliberate steps toward becoming the godly man God has called you to be. This journey hasn't been easy, but it has been worth it.

You've grown in your relationship with Christ, strengthened your faith, and developed lasting habits that will guide you for the rest of your life. You've learned the importance of brotherhood, accountability, and sharing your faith with others. Most importantly, you've begun to leave a legacy—not just for yourself, but for your family, your community, and future generations.

As you move forward, remember that this study is not the end of your journey. Continue applying the principles you've learned and stay committed to living out your faith daily. Trust God in every trial and rely on His strength in every spiritual battle. Lead your family with courage, serve your church faithfully, and mentor the next generation. Find other men you can take through this study and become the disciple- maker god has called you to be.

May God bless you as you continue to pursue Him with all your heart, mind, and strength. The world needs godly men like you, men who will stand firm in their faith, live boldly for Christ, and make a lasting impact for His Kingdom.

**You have been called, equipped, and now sent out to live as a man of God. Keep pressing on!**

**Final Challenge: Start Your Own Group**

As you complete this study, you've taken an important step in growing as a godly man. But this is not the end of your journey—it's just the beginning. God has equipped you with biblical truths, spiritual disciplines, and leadership principles not just for your own life, but to share with others. You are now called to take what you've learned and pass it on to other men, creating a ripple effect that impacts lives, families, and communities for Christ.

Jesus' final words to His disciples were a challenge: *"Go, therefore, and make disciples of all the nations..."* (Matthew 28:19). That command is for you, too. The world desperately needs godly men who are willing to lead, teach, and invest in others. Now is the time to step up and start your own group of men. Whether it's a small gathering at your home, a coffee shop Bible study, or a men's group at your church, God can use you to disciple others and multiply the impact of this study.

Here's the challenge:

1. **Pray** – Ask God to guide you and bring the right men into your life who are ready for this journey.
2. **Invite** – Reach out to men who need encouragement, growth, and brotherhood. Be bold in asking them to join you.
3. **Lead** – Use what you've learned in this study to guide others. Be transparent, honest, and committed to helping them grow.
4. **Multiply** – Encourage the men in your group to one day start their own groups, creating a cycle of discipleship that continues for generations.

Men, the world needs you to be leaders, disciples, and disciple-makers. Will you take the next step? Will you rise to the challenge of mentoring and leading other men in the faith? You have the tools, you have the calling—now it's time to act. The legacy of godly manhood starts with you.

# ABOUT THE AUTHOR: JODY BURKEEN

Jody Burkeen is a devoted husband, father, pastor, and author passionate about equipping men and families to live godly lives in an increasingly ungodly world. Married for 34 years, Jody cherishes his role as a husband to his wife, Nan, and as a father to their four children.

With a Master's degree in Theology, Jody combines deep biblical knowledge with practical application in his teaching and writing. As the founder of *Man Up God's Way*, a ministry dedicated to challenging men to step into their God-given roles, Jody's life mission is to inspire others to live boldly for Christ.

His straightforward and passionate approach has made a profound impact through his books, devotions, and sermons, empowering readers and listeners to embrace the truth of God's Word and transform their lives. Whether in the pulpit, at home, or on the page, Jody remains steadfast in his commitment to glorify God in all he does.

## My Personal Mission Statement

As a man committed to God's purpose for my life, I will strive daily to live in alignment with His design, embracing my identity in Christ as a new creation. I will seek to lead my family with integrity, humility, and love, and will take responsibility for my role as a spiritual leader in my home, church, and community. I commit to reading God's Word, praying fervently, and repenting of any sin that God reveals, trusting in His grace to shape me into a man of faith, strength, and courage.

I will live by faith, not by the desires of the flesh, and will pursue holiness in all areas of life, setting a godly example for others to follow. I will invest in the spiritual growth of others by discipling men and standing firm in my faith, even in the face of trials. My mission is to leave a legacy of faith, demonstrating the love and power of Christ in all I do, so that my family, those I lead, and the generations to come will know and follow Him.

**Life Verse**- is a specific passage or verse from the Bible that holds deep personal significance for an individual. It often serves as a guiding principle, source of encouragement, or anchor in our faith journey. I choose a life verse because it resonates with my personal experiences, spiritual goals, and personal challenges I face. It becomes a lens through which I view my life, decisions, and relationship with God.

> **Romans 8:6**- *"For the mind set on the flesh is death, but the mind set on the Spirit is life and peace"*

Made in United States
Cleveland, OH
19 March 2026

34632752R00168